D1402139

This book is from
the kitchen library of

_____

_____

BY ART GINSBURG, **Mr. Food**®

The Mr. Food® Cookbook, OOH IT'S SO GOOD!!® (1990)

Mr. Food® Cooks Like Mama (1992)

Mr. Food® Cooks Chicken (1993)

Mr. Food® Cooks Pasta (1993)

Mr. Food® Makes Dessert (1993)

Mr. Food® Cooks Real American (1994)

Mr. Food®'s Favorite Cookies (1994)

Mr. Food®'s Quick and Easy Side Dishes (1995)

Mr. Food® Grills It All in a Snap (1995)

Mr. Food®'s Fun Kitchen Tips and Shortcuts (and Recipes, Too!) (1995)

Mr. Food®'s Old World Cooking Made Easy (1995)

"Help, Mr. Food®! Company's Coming!" (1995)

Mr. Food® Pizza 1-2-3 (1996)

Mr. Food® Meat Around the Table (1996)

Mr. Food® Simply Chocolate (1996)

Mr. Food® A Little Lighter (1996)

Mr. Food® From My Kitchen to Yours: Stories and Recipes from Home (1996)

Mr. Food® Easy Tex-Mex (1997)

Mr. Food® One Pot, One Meal (1997)

Mr. Food® Cool Cravings (1997)

Mr. Food®'s Italian Kitchen (1997)

Mr. Food®'s Simple Southern Favorites (1997)

A Mr. Food® Christmas: Homemade and Hassle-Free (1998)

Mr. Food® Cooking by the Calendar: Fifty-two Weeks of Year-Round Favorites (1999)

Mr. Food®'s Meals in Minutes (1999)

Mr. Food®'s Good Times, Good Food Cookbook (1999)

Mr. Food®'s Restaurant Favorites (1999)

Mr. Food®'s

Meals in Minutes

Art Ginsburg
Mr. Food®

WILLIAM MORROW AND COMPANY, INC. • NEW YORK

Copyright © 1999 by Cogin, Inc.

Photographs copyright © 1999 by the Hal Silverman Studio

All rights reserved. No part of this book may be reproduced or utilized in any form or by any means, electronic or mechanical, including photocopying, recording, or by any information storage or retrieval system, without permission in writing from the Publisher. Inquiries should be addressed to Permissions Department, William Morrow and Company, Inc., 1350 Avenue of the Americas, New York, N.Y. 10019.

It is the policy of William Morrow and Company, Inc., and its imprints and affiliates, recognizing the importance of preserving what has been written, to print the books we publish on acid-free paper, and we exert our best efforts to that end.

Library of Congress Cataloging-in-Publication data is available.
ISBN 0-688-15088-8

Printed in the United States of America

First Edition

2 3 4 5 6 7 8 9 10

BOOK DESIGN BY MICHAEL MENDELSOHN AT MM DESIGN 2000, INC.

www.williammorrow.com
www.mrfood.com

Dedicated to
all the moms and dads
who encourage communication and togetherness
by sharing regular family meals.

Acknowledgments

Now's the time I get to thank everybody who worked around the clock with me to bring you my fastest cookbook yet, *Mr. Food's Meals in Minutes.*

Just like a good old dependable grandfather clock, my test kitchen staff is always on hand to share their timesaving ideas and tasty recipes. What a great team I've got in the creative Patty Rosenthal, the attentive-to-detail Janice Bruce, the enthusiastic Cheryl Gerber and spirited Cela Goodhue, and the inventive Gerri Seinberg. Joe Peppi keeps everything moving along on time by overseeing the work done both in the test kitchen and by Charlie Tallant, who cheerfully documents all our preparation steps. And I can't forget to say *gracias* to Dio Gomez for keeping our kitchen shining so brightly.

I don't know what I'd do without the assistance and talents of Howard Rosenthal and Caryl Ginsburg Fantel, who work with me hour after hour, day after day to keep my books and so many other projects on track, along with the imaginative and detail-minded support of Larissa Lalka.

Just as clocks have many different faces and functions, so does my dedicated office staff. There's our meticulous stopwatch, better known as my son Steve, who keeps time and order by overseeing the many Mr. Food ventures. Then there's our alarm clock, Chet Rosenbaum, who, along with his able assistant, Carol Ginsburg, keeps our business affairs in line; licensing director Tom Palombo and his assistant, Heidi Triveri; amiable Station Relations Coordinator Alice Palombo; Marilyn Ruderman, my assistant, who keeps all my days organized;

Helayne Rosenblum, my capable and clever script assistant; Rhonda Weiss, my editorial assistant, who has an unmatched way with words; Beth Ives, our timely customer service manager; and Robin Steiner, our administrative assistant, who's always ready to jump in and help out with anything that needs doing. I certainly can't forget to thank my son Chuck, and my wife, Ethel, who, thankfully, is always—and has always been—in the right place at the right time.

Okay, it's time. For what? To thank the rest of the folks who are part of the Mr. Food success. I'm grateful for the support of my agent, Bill Adler, who works so closely with the team at publisher William Morrow. And there are lots of people to mention at Morrow, too: Bill Wright, President and CEO of the Hearst Book Group; Michael Murphy, Publisher and Senior Vice President; and Senior Editor Zachary Schisgal. There's also Richard Aquan and Nikki Basilone. And, of course, everybody at the Hal Silverman Studio came through for us again, as did Michael Mendelsohn of MM Design 2000, Inc. My thanks to you all!

And now, as the kitchen timer rings, I want to thank you, my viewers and readers, for allowing me to share so many fun moments in the kitchen with you. You can be sure we're gonna have lots more time together to explore even more ways to say "OOH IT'S SO GOOD!!®"

Contents

Acknowledgments   vii

Introduction   xi

A Moderate Approach   xiii

A Note About Packaged Foods   xvii

Breakfast on the Go   3

Brunch   15

Lunch: Soups, Salads, and Sandwiches 33

Snack Attack   61

Family Dinner   89

Dinner for Two   121

Dessert   139

Index   167

*I*ntroduction

Okay, here it is . . . the fastest cookbook around. Really. And it's because of you, my readers. You see, when I started gathering ideas for this, my latest cookbook, I figured who better to ask than the biggest Mr. Food fans? So here's what happened when I took a survey to ask what you'd like to see most in a Mr. Food cookbook.

One day, a couple of weeks after we mailed the surveys, I walked into my office holding a big bag of fresh tomatoes, peppers, and onions from my favorite farmers' market. And I nearly tripped over a giant U.S. Mail bag! After I regained my balance, I saw that the bag was overflowing with completed surveys. Why, I was so excited, my bag of produce almost became instant salsa! As it turned out, thousands of my fans had sent me their comments.

We spent days reading them, and more time tabulating them (thank goodness for computers!), and the end result was overwhelming. May I have a drum roll, please? Here's what you told me you want more than anything: fast home-cooked meals that don't require lots of ingredients. To me, that meant recipes that get you in and out of the kitchen in 30 minutes or less and have no more than eight ingredients. Oh, yes—you absolutely want food that tastes good, too.

So I challenged myself. I decided that every recipe in this book had to be extra-easy and superfast. **When I say it takes 30 minutes or less, that includes preparation *and* cooking time.** Other cookbooks make similar promises, but usually when you read the recipes, you'll find ones such as a "20-minute" pot roast that actually has to cook for 3½ hours and a "5-minute" frozen pie that needs to be frozen for 4 hours or more before serving. **And when I say eight ingredients, I**

mean eight. Not eight *plus* salt, pepper, sugar, oil, flour, and any other traditional standby ingredients.

Now, if you have all the time in the world, don't mind driving around to specialty stores looking for exotic ingredients, and love to spend hours preparing meals, then this cookbook isn't for you. On the other hand, if you balance a busy schedule of family, work, school, and other activities—or you just don't want to spend your time over a stove full of pots and pans—then get ready, 'cause this book is gonna be a lifesaver for you again and again.

They say the proof is in the pudding. And in this case, it's in everything from breakfast to dinner, brunch to dessert . . . and all those other times when we eat. So no matter where those clock hands are pointing when your stomach starts grumbling, it'll be just a matter of minutes before you're ready to dig into any of the timesaving, lip-smacking "OOH IT'S SO GOOD!!®"

A Moderate Approach

Quick cooking doesn't mean we stop watching what we eat. Here are a few ideas to help you enjoy healthier eating without sacrificing taste or flavor.

Chicken In most recipes, you can substitute boneless, skinless chicken breasts for whole chicken or parts. Remember that boneless breasts are generally thinner, so they'll cook more quickly than bone-in parts; adjust your cooking times accordingly.

Dairy Let's look to our supermarket dairy case for some reduced-fat, low-fat, or fat-free alternatives. For instance, there's low-fat milk for our soups and sauces, instead of heavy cream. (Evaporated skim milk will work, too.)

Cream Cheese Easy—use light or fat-free cream cheese!

Mozzarella Cheese Many of the low-fat and part-skim mozzarella cheeses taste just as good as the traditional types. They're perfect alternatives, plus you can also usually cut down on the amount you use. (We can often reduce the amount of cheese we sprinkle on the tops of casseroles without anybody even noticing!)

Parmesan Cheese Parmesan is an excellent choice when watching fat and calories, since its strong flavor means that a little goes a long way! (It's the same with Romano cheese.)

Ricotta Cheese

For rich taste while still watching fat, in most ricotta recipes you can use half regular ricotta and half light or fat-free ricotta. Or, don't hesitate to use all light or fat-free. The choice is yours.

Sour Cream

I often use light versions without missing any flavor, but because sour cream varies widely by brand, I recommend trying several brands until you find the one with the taste and consistency you like best.

Whipped Cream

Many desserts call for whipped cream or whipped topping. To watch calories and fat with those, we've got great choices available with reduced-fat and nonfat whipped toppings. You may need to increase the flavoring or sugar a bit, though, depending on the recipe.

Dressings

Add a splash of vinegar or citrus juice—lemon, lime, or orange—to dressings or marinades (and vegetables, poultry, and almost anything else, too) in place of some of the traditional oil.

Eggs

In many cases, we can replace whole eggs with egg whites. (Two egg whites equal one whole egg.) And, yes, in most recipes, you can go ahead and replace eggs altogether with egg substitute. (It's usually available near the eggs in the refrigerated section of the supermarket.) However, I don't recommend using egg substitute when coating foods for breading. Breading doesn't stick to it very well.

Mayonnaise   When it comes to mayonnaise, there are lighter varieties available, too. And when using it in a salad, mix it in just before serving . . . you can usually get by with using less that way. Or sometimes I use a combination of half mayonnaise and half low-fat yogurt. It does the trick, too!

Meats   • Choose lean cuts of meat and trim away any visible fat before preparing.

• Serve moderate-sized portions, such as 3 to 4 ounces of cooked meat (4 to 6 ounces raw) per adult. (That's about the size of a deck of playing cards.)

• Choose cooking methods (like roasting on a rack, broiling, and grilling) that allow fat to drip away during cooking.

• Remove the layer of fat that rises to the top of soups, stews, and the pan juices of roasts. Chilling makes this a breeze, so it's even easier to do with dishes that are made ahead and chilled before being reheated. Or, a timesaving tip for removing fat from soups and stews is simply to add a few ice cubes to the warm cooked dish. As soon as the fat sticks to the cubes, remove them, and the fat will come out right along with them!

Ground Beef
and Pork   • Select a very lean blend, preferably with a 90 to 10 ratio of lean meat to fat. (Regular ground beef and pork usually have a 70 to 30 ratio.)

- If browning ground beef or pork before adding it to a recipe, after browning, place it in a strainer and rinse it with warm water, then drain and continue as directed. This should remove most of the excess fat.

- In most recipes, you can replace ground beef or pork with turkey. Keep in mind, though, that ground turkey needs more seasoning than beef or pork.

Sausage

Many markets now offer a variety of lean sausages. This means that there's less fat mixed in with the meat when the sausage is made. Other alternatives to traditional pork and beef sausages are turkey and chicken sausages. Whichever way you go, be sure to read the nutrition label so you know your fat and calorie savings.

Nuts

When a recipe calls for nuts, don't be afraid to cut down the amount. Usually we can cut the amount in half and still get great flavor and texture.

Oils

Select oils such as canola or safflower for frying; they're lower in saturated fat than other types.

Sauces

Have you seen all the prepared sauces available in the supermarket lately? Not only are there lots of flavors available, but most manufacturers are offering sauces that have less fat and calories, and even ones with less sodium, too. Some of these may be thinner than our "regular" sauces, so you may want to use a bit less of them than normal.

Soups   Canned soups are a great beginning for sauces and casseroles. If we choose lighter or reduced-fat or reduced-sodium versions, we can sure save calories and cut down on fat and sodium.

How you eat is almost as important as *what* you eat. So follow these basic common-sense eating habits:

- Eat regularly scheduled meals and limit eating between meals. There are two rules of thumb on this: Eat three scheduled meals a day and limit eating between meals *OR* eat five to six light meals throughout the day. But don't do both, and *never* stuff yourself!

- Try not to eat within two hours of bedtime.

- Watch portion sizes! Smaller portions mean fewer calories, so serve yourself only as much food as you think you'll eat. It's okay to leave some on your plate, too.

- With all the time we'll save by using the recipes in this book, we should try to make time for a walk, a bike ride, or something else active each day. Let's not forget to take a moderate approach with exercise, too.

A Note About Packaged Foods

Packaged food sizes may vary by brand. Generally, the sizes indicated in these recipes are average sizes. If you can't find the exact package size listed in the ingredients, whatever package is closest in size will usually do the trick.

Mr. Food®'s

Meals
in
Minutes

Breakfast on the Go

Some people say breakfast is the most important meal of the day. If that's the case, why do so many of us skip it? Here's why: between the household chores, the daily carpool, and all our regular paperwork, who has the time to make, much less eat, a breakfast that's not only healthy, but also quick and satisfying? And if we eat it at all, most of us rely on cold cereal or doughnuts as our kick start to the morning.

Guess what! Things are about to change in our homes, so start the clock and get ready for some of the tastiest and fastest breakfasts out there.

Breakfast on the Go

French Toast Sticks   5

Morning Pizza   6

Apple Pie Toast   7

3–2–1 Power Bars   8

Breakfast Cookies   9

Raspberry Toaster Cakes   10

Sausage Pancake Muffins   11

Cinnamon Pecan Muffins   12

Mocha Icee   13

French Toast Sticks

16 STICKS

4 eggs
½ cup milk
¼ cup maple syrup
1 cup confectioners' sugar
½ teaspoon ground cinnamon
8 hot dog rolls, cut lengthwise in half
3 tablespoons butter

In the past, French toast always meant sticky hands and mouths and lots of napkins. Not anymore, 'cause these have the flavorings and syrup already cooked in. Nope, there's no need to sprinkle them with cinnamon . . . it's in there. And forget about drizzling 'em with syrup, 'cause that's in there, too. The bonus? It's all wrapped in one neat package.

In a shallow dish, beat the eggs, milk, maple syrup, confectioners' sugar, and cinnamon until well blended. Dip the hot dog roll halves into the egg mixture, coating completely. Melt 1 tablespoon butter in a large skillet over medium heat. Cook the rolls a few at a time for 2 to 3 minutes per side, or until golden, adding more butter as needed. Serve immediately, or allow to cool, then cover and chill until ready to serve. Reheat in a preheated 350°F. oven for 3 to 5 minutes, or until heated through.

TIMESAVING TIP:
This is just the thing to make the night before serving so the next morning you can simply reheat it in the oven or toaster oven (*not* the microwave) for a hot breakfast treat in no time.

Morning Pizza

We've all seen the different kinds of pizzas that are available at our local supermarkets and take-out restaurants. Well, here's another variation—breakfast pizza. It's covered with fluffy scrambled eggs and crispy bacon and smothered in melted cheese for a true breakfast delight. Just slice and go!

6 TO 8 SLICES

1 tablespoon butter

6 eggs, beaten

One 12-inch prepared pizza shell

⅓ cup real bacon bits

3 slices (2¼ ounces) American cheese, cut into ½-inch strips

Preheat the oven to 450°F. Melt the butter in a large skillet over medium-low heat. Add the eggs and scramble until firm. Place the pizza shell on a pizza pan, spoon the scrambled eggs over the top, and sprinkle with the bacon bits. Place the strips of cheese over the bacon and bake for 7 to 8 minutes, or until the crust is crisp and brown. Slice and serve.

SO MANY OPTIONS!
Substitute any of your favorite pizza toppings, from canned mushrooms and olives to pepperoni, for the bacon bits.

Apple Pie Toast

6 SLICES

6 slices cinnamon-raisin bread
1 can (21 ounces) apple pie filling, drained
6 slices (1 ounce each) sharp Cheddar cheese

Why settle for plain old toast and jam when we can sink our teeth into a juicy breakfast-style apple pie? Okay, so maybe it's not a real pie, but once you take a bite, your imagination will have you believing it is!

Preheat the broiler. Place the cinnamon-raisin bread on a baking sheet and lightly toast under the broiler. Remove from the broiler and top each bread slice with an equal amount of apple pie filling and a cheese slice. Broil for 2 to 3 minutes, or until the filling is heated through and the cheese is melted. Serve immediately.

HELPFUL HINT:
Can't find sliced Cheddar cheese? Slice it from a block or, even easier, just sprinkle on a cup (4 ounces) of shredded Cheddar cheese.

3–2–1 Power Bars

Everybody can use an extra boost in the morning, especially on Mondays! Go ahead and try a 3–2–1 power bar . . . but be prepared to blast into the busy week ahead.

15 TO 18 BARS

3 cups granola with fruit and nuts

2 cups Rice Krispies® cereal

1 cup sweetened dried cranberries

3 tablespoons butter

24 marshmallows

Coat a 9" × 13" baking dish with nonstick cooking spray. In a large bowl, combine the granola, cereal, and cran-berries; mix well. Melt the butter in a soup pot over low heat. Add the marshmallows and cook until melted and smooth, stirring constantly. Remove from the heat and stir in the granola mixture until well combined. Spoon the mixture into the baking dish and pat down evenly. Let sit for 15 minutes, or until firm, then cut into bars. Serve, or store in an airtight container until ready to serve.

HELPFUL HINT:
To give these the most flavor, choose a granola that has lots of fruit and nuts.

Breakfast Cookies

ABOUT 3 DOZEN COOKIES

4½ cups granola cereal
with raisins, divided

½ cup (1 stick) butter, softened

½ cup firmly packed light brown sugar

1 envelope (1¼ ounces) vanilla
instant breakfast drink mix

1 egg

¾ cup all-purpose flour

¼ teaspoon baking powder

½ teaspoon ground
cinnamon

Instead of serving individual breakfast shakes and granola, why not combine them in the form of a tasty cookie? Just wait until the kids hear that cookies are on the breakfast menu! Sure, we can keep it our secret that these are chock-full of stuff that's good for them.

Preheat the oven to 350°F. Place 1½ cups cereal in a shallow dish, breaking up the larger pieces; set aside. In a large bowl, beat the butter, brown sugar, instant breakfast mix, and egg until smooth. Add the flour, baking powder, and cinnamon; beat until thoroughly combined. Add the remaining 3 cups cereal; beat until well mixed. Form into 1-inch balls and coat in the reserved cereal, rolling to coat completely. Place on cookie sheets 2 inches apart and bake for 12 to 14 minutes, or until firm and light golden. Serve warm, or allow to cool and store in an airtight container.

HELPFUL HINT:
Thanks to the instant breakfast drink mix, these cookies are full of vitamins and minerals. It's easy to change the flavor of the cookies simply by using a different flavored breakfast drink mix.

Raspberry Toaster Cakes

Instead of spending a lot of money on expensive pastry snacks at the supermarket, why not make them at home for a lot less? They'll be brimming with a lot more fruity taste, so it's a great way to get the kids to help out for a fun afternoon project. Then, when morning comes, they can enjoy the "fruits" of their labors.

8 TOASTER CAKES

1 package (15 ounces) refrigerated folded pie crusts (2 crusts)

½ cup raspberry preserves

Preheat the oven to 450°F. Unfold the pie crusts and cut each into 4 equal wedges along the fold lines. Place an equal amount of preserves in the center of each wedge. Brush the edges of each wedge with water and fold lengthwise in half to form a triangle. Seal the edges and crimp with a fork. Bake on an ungreased baking sheet for 8 to 10 minutes, or until golden. Serve, or allow to cool completely, then cover and chill until ready to serve. Reheat in the oven or toaster.

TIMESAVING TIP: If you make these in advance, you can have homemade toaster snacks ready anytime—in *no* time!

Sausage Pancake Muffins

1 DOZEN MUFFINS

2 cups packaged pancake
and waffle mix

2 eggs

1 cup milk

½ cup club soda

1 tablespoon vegetable oil

4 heat-and-serve beef sausages,
chopped (half of a 5.2-ounce package)

¼ cup pancake syrup

Mmm, there's nothing like one of those big old-fashioned breakfasts that Mom used to make. You know, a plate filled with scrambled eggs, pancakes with syrup, and bacon or sausage. But honestly, who has the time to make all that? We've certainly got time to make these sausage pancake muffins, and they really do capture the flavor.

Preheat the oven to 350°F. Coat a 12-cup muffin tin with nonstick cooking spray. In a large bowl, combine the pancake mix, eggs, milk, club soda, and oil; mix well. Pour evenly into the muffin cups and sprinkle with the sausage. Bake for 20 to 25 minutes, or until a wooden toothpick inserted in the center comes out clean. Remove from the oven and brush the tops with the pancake syrup. Serve warm.

FOR A CHANGE OF PACE:
Instead of sausage, these can also be made with fresh blueberries or peeled and chopped apples.

Cinnamon Pecan Muffins

It seems like we're always rushed in the morning! Now, when it comes to breakfast, we can have this yummy combination of cinnamon buns and an old favorite, coffee cake. Oh—did I mention they're ready in minutes?

1 DOZEN MUFFINS

½ cup chopped pecans

⅓ cup firmly packed
light brown sugar

1 teaspoon ground cinnamon

2 cups biscuit baking mix

⅓ cup granulated sugar

1 egg

⅔ cup milk

¼ cup sour cream

Preheat the oven to 400°F. Coat a 12-cup muffin tin with nonstick cooking spray. In a large bowl, combine the pecans, brown sugar, and cinnamon; mix well. Measure out and reserve ⅓ cup of the mixture. Add the remaining ingredients to the remaining pecan mixture; stir until just moistened. Spoon evenly into the muffin cups. Sprinkle with the reserved pecan mixture and bake for 15 to 18 minutes, or until golden and a wooden toothpick inserted in the center comes out clean. Serve warm, or allow to cool slightly, then remove to a wire rack to cool completely.

TO FANCY IT UP:
Top the chopped pecan mixture on each pancake with a pecan half.

Mocha Icee

**ABOUT 1 QUART;
3 TO 4 SERVINGS**

¾ cup milk

¼ cup instant coffee granules

¼ cup sugar

1 envelope (1¼ ounces) chocolate instant breakfast drink mix (see Note)

3 cups ice cubes

When I drive to work, it seems like all the other drivers are drinking coffee from travel mugs. Sure, I'd love to drink my coffee in the car, but it's just too darned hot—and dangerous. That's why I created this creamy smoothie—so I could have my coffee and drink it, too.

In a blender, combine all the ingredients except the ice; blend until well mixed. Add the ice and blend until well combined and slushy. Serve immediately.

> **SO MANY OPTIONS!**
> Sure, you can use an envelope of vanilla instant breakfast drink mix if you want a vanilla-flavored coffee drink.

Brunch

At one time or another, all of us have enjoyed a leisurely weekend brunch at home. You know how relaxing it is to spend the morning catching up on reading and snacking on yummy treats like muffins hot out of the oven, fresh fruit, and home-made omelets. On those lazy days, before we know it, it's noon and we're still in our pajamas!

Unfortunately, we don't often have spare time to spend that way anymore. There's grocery shopping to be done, dry cleaning to be picked up, and we can't forget about the kids needing to be taken to soccer practice, Sunday school, and all. With all that to do (and those are just the morning activities!), the weekend brunch seems to have gotten lost in the shuffle . . . and that's too bad!

Even though we all have busy schedules, family time is very important, so why not schedule a family brunch once or twice a month—and accept no excuses for missing it? Now don't worry, you won't spend all morning in the kitchen cooking, 'cause I've prepared a bunch of shortcut recipes to make brunch an extra-special but extra-easy treat for all.

Brunch

Mini Ham and Cheese Quiches   18

Crab Puffs   19

Vegetable Frittata   20

Skillet Home Fries and Eggs   21

Shortcut Omelets   22

Bull's-eye Eggs   23

Creamed Chipped Beef   24

Biscuits with Sausage Gravy   25

Bandito Burrito Bake   26

Pecan Sticky Buns   27

Chocolate-Banana Baked French Toast   28

Baked Chocolate Chip Pancakes   29

Open-faced Strawberry Cheese Danish   30

Shortcut Fresh OJ   31

Mini Ham and Cheese Quiches

Weekend brunches are for relaxing, not cooking. That's why I came up with a quiche that's ready in under 20 minutes. Yup, that's about half the baking time of traditional quiches.

1 DOZEN QUICHES

12 round butter-flavored crackers
2 eggs, beaten
1 cup (½ pint) heavy cream
2 cups (8 ounces) shredded Swiss cheese
⅓ cup chopped deli ham

Preheat the oven to 400°F. Coat a 12-cup muffin tin with nonstick cooking spray. Place one cracker in the bottom of each muffin cup. In a medium bowl, combine the remaining ingredients; mix well and spoon into the muffin cups. Bake for 18 to 20 minutes, or until golden. Serve immediately.

HELPFUL HINT:
No deli ham on hand? Use real bacon bits instead to make mini quiche lorraines.

Crab Puffs

8 MUFFIN PUFFS

4 English muffins, split

2 cans (6 ounces each) crabmeat, drained and flaked

1 package (8 ounces) cream cheese, softened

¼ cup mayonnaise

1 teaspoon spicy brown mustard

4 scallions, thinly sliced

⅛ teaspoon black pepper

Creamy crabmeat piled high on an English muffin and broiled . . . now that's brunch at its finest. It's so fancy sounding, but when you see how easy it is, you'll fall for it hook, line, and sinker.

Preheat the broiler. Place the muffin halves on a baking sheet and lightly toast under the broiler. In a medium bowl, combine the remaining ingredients; mix well and spread evenly over the muffin halves. Broil for 4 to 5 minutes, or until slightly puffed and golden. Serve immediately.

SO MANY OPTIONS!
The same crab mixture can be used on crackers and baked to create bite-sized crab puff hors d'oeuvres.

Vegetable Frittata

Did you know that a frittata is a type of omelet? Frittatas have their flavoring ingredients mixed and cooked right into the eggs, and they're not folded like omelets. This frittata happens to be packed with hash browns, peppers, onions, and, of course, a whole bunch of ooey, gooey melted cheese.

4 TO 6 SERVINGS

¼ cup vegetable oil

2 cups frozen Southern-style hash brown potatoes, thawed

8 eggs

2 cups (8 ounces) *shredded* Parmesan cheese

½ teaspoon salt

½ teaspoon black pepper

1 package (16 ounces) frozen bell pepper and onion mix, thawed and drained

Heat the oil in a large skillet over high heat. Add the potatoes and cook for 12 to 15 minutes, or until soft, stirring occasionally. Meanwhile, in a large bowl, whisk together the eggs, cheese, salt, and black pepper. Stir in the bell pepper and onion mix, then pour over the potatoes. Reduce the heat to medium, cover, and cook for 8 to 10 minutes, or until the eggs are completely set. Cut into wedges and serve.

SO MANY OPTIONS!
Sure, you can use different frozen vegetables if you'd prefer, or even sauté some fresh vegetables to add to the egg mixture.

Skillet Home Fries and Eggs

6 SERVINGS

½ cup (1 stick) butter

1 red or green bell pepper (or ½ red and ½ green), diced

1 small onion, chopped

1 pound frozen hash brown potatoes

½ teaspoon salt

¼ teaspoon black pepper

6 eggs

Even though we like to spend extra time with our breakfast on the weekend, we shouldn't have to spend extra time in the kitchen getting it ready! Just grab a skillet and in no time you'll have a diner breakfast that's guaranteed to get them going.

Melt the butter in a large skillet over high heat. Add the bell pepper and onion and sauté for 2 minutes. Add the hash brown potatoes, salt, and black pepper and stir until well combined. Cook for 10 to 12 minutes, or until golden, stirring frequently. Reduce the heat to medium. Using a spoon, make 6 evenly spaced indentations about ½ inch deep in the mixture. Crack the eggs one at a time and place each in an indentation. Cover the skillet and cook for 7 to 9 minutes, or until the eggs are set and cooked as desired. Serve immediately.

TIMESAVING TIP:
To remove stubborn dried-on eggs from utensils and plates, run cold water—not hot—over them before washing. That'll make cleanup a breeze.

TO KEEP THINGS EXCITING . . .
Add a splash of salsa or hot pepper sauce to the home fries for extra zing.

Shortcut Omelets

Until now, making four different omelets meant using four different pans, or cooking each omelet separately. Isn't it time we took a shortcut? It's one that'll have them scrambling to the table in no time.

Melt the butter in a large skillet over medium heat. Add the onion and sauté for 1 to 2 minutes, or until tender. Add the chilies, mushrooms, and eggs and scramble the eggs for 3 to 4 minutes, or until soft scrambled. In the skillet, divide the scrambled egg mixture into 4 equal servings and top each with a slice of cheese. Cover and cook for 1 to 2 minutes, or until the cheese is melted and the eggs are cooked to the desired consistency. Serve immediately.

4 SERVINGS

1 tablespoon butter

½ small onion, diced

1 can (4½ ounces) chopped green chilies, drained

1 can (4 ounces) mushroom stems and pieces, drained

6 eggs, beaten

4 slices (3 ounces) Mexican-style American cheese

HELPFUL HINT:
Make this part of a buffet and serve it with two or three other selections from this chapter.

Bull's-eye Eggs

2 SERVINGS

4 slices white or potato bread

2 tablespoons butter, melted

4 eggs

Eggs piled high on top of toast are a longtime breakfast favorite, and with this easy version, we eliminate an entire step. Yup, we bake the eggs and toast the bread all together. The result is a one-dish wonder.

Preheat the oven to 375°F. Coat a 10" × 15" rimmed baking sheet with nonstick cooking spray. Using a 2½-inch biscuit cutter or a knife, cut a circle out of the center of each slice of bread. Place the bread slices on the baking sheet and brush with half of the melted butter, then flip and brush the other sides with the remaining melted butter. Crack the eggs one at a time and place one in the center hole of each bread slice. Bake for 12 to 14 minutes, or until the bread is golden and the eggs are cooked through. Serve immediately.

TO KEEP THINGS EXCITING . . .
Give the kids an extra-special treat by serving them one slice sunny-side up and a second slice turned over, so the eggs look as if they're "winking." And maybe make mouths and noses out of the circles cut from the centers of the bread.

Creamed Chipped Beef

My frequent travels often take me to small towns, and it's there that I've found some of the best diners. It's not unusual to see chipped beef as one of the daily specials. What a tasty treat it is once in a while. Of course, the best treat is how easy it is to make.

4 SERVINGS

2 jars (2¼ ounces each) sliced dried beef, cut into ½-inch strips

2 tablespoons butter

2 tablespoons all-purpose flour

¼ teaspoon onion powder

¼ teaspoon black pepper

1 cup milk

1 teaspoon Worcestershire sauce

4 slices white bread, toasted and cut diagonally in half

Place the beef in a medium bowl and add enough warm water to cover. Soak for 2 minutes; drain, rinse, and drain again. In a medium skillet, combine the beef, butter, flour, onion powder, and pepper over medium heat. Cook until the butter melts, stirring constantly. Add the milk and Worcestershire sauce; mix well. Bring to a boil and cook for 2 to 3 minutes, or until the sauce is thickened, stirring constantly. Spoon an equal amount of the beef mixture over each piece of toast. Serve immediately.

> **HELPFUL HINT:**
> Since dried beef is so salty, I like to soak and rinse it first to remove some of the salt.

Biscuits with Sausage Gravy

4 TO 6 SERVINGS

Just making true Southern country-style gravy and biscuits can take an entire morning . . . and we don't usually have that much time! So I bet y'all are gonna love this shortcut recipe that's great as is or served with fluffy scrambled eggs and hominy grits.

1 package (7½ ounces) refrigerated biscuits (10 biscuits)

1 tube (16 ounces) hot pork sausage (see Hint)

3 tablespoons all-purpose flour

1 tablespoon Worcestershire sauce

1½ cups milk

1 tablespoon chopped fresh parsley

Bake the biscuits according to the package directions. Meanwhile, in a large skillet, cook the sausage over medium-high heat for 6 to 8 minutes, or until no pink remains, stirring to crumble the meat. Add the flour; mix well. Add the Worcestershire sauce and milk; mix well. Cook for 2 to 4 minutes, or until the gravy thickens, stirring constantly. Serve over the biscuits and sprinkle with the chopped parsley.

HELPFUL HINT:
Make sure to use the hot pork sausage that comes in a tube, not hot Italian pork sausage from the meat case.

Bandito Burrito Bake

Ever tried breakfast burritos? They're really popular these days, so why not try this simple baked version? I know it's gonna give you reason to shout, "Olé!"

1 jar (16 ounces) salsa, divided

1 tablespoon butter

1 small onion, finely chopped

8 eggs, beaten

1 can (11 ounces) Mexican-style corn, drained

Six 8-inch flour tortillas

2 cups (8 ounces) shredded Mexican cheese blend

Preheat the oven to 425°F. Coat a 9" × 13" baking dish with non-stick cooking spray. Spread 1 cup salsa over the bottom of the baking dish. Melt the butter in a large skillet over medium-high heat. Add the onion and sauté for 1 to 2 minutes, or until tender. Add the eggs and corn and scramble the eggs for 1 to 2 minutes, or until firm. Place an equal amount of the egg mixture across the center of each tortilla and roll up. Place seam side down in the baking dish. Drizzle the remaining salsa over the tortillas and sprinkle with the cheese. Bake for 10 to 12 minutes, or until bubbly and the cheese has melted. Serve immediately.

GREAT GO-ALONG:
Make a pot of strong coffee and add a bit of coffee-flavored liqueur to each cup to really wake up Mexican-style.

TIMESAVING TIP:
The fastest way to clean your coffee maker is to simply run it through a brewing cycle using white vinegar instead of water. Then run a few more cycles with just water.

Pecan Sticky Buns

9 BUNS

½ cup firmly packed light brown sugar, divided

3 tablespoons butter, melted, divided

1 tablespoon light corn syrup

¾ cup chopped pecans, divided

1 package (8 ounces) refrigerated crescent rolls (8 rolls)

1 teaspoon ground cinnamon

Imagine the taste of fresh sticky buns hot from the oven. Now imagine the same buns ready in under 30 minutes. There's no need to imagine, 'cause they're a reality! And wait until you take a bite. I don't know what the best part is—the melted brown sugar, the chopped pecans, or the cinnamon—so I'll have to cast my vote for the whole package!

Preheat the oven to 375°F. Coat an 8-inch square baking dish with nonstick cooking spray. In a small bowl, combine ¼ cup brown sugar, 2 tablespoons butter, and the corn syrup; mix well, until smooth, then spread over the bottom of the baking dish. Sprinkle with ½ cup pecans. Unroll the crescent dough and press the seams together to form one large rectangle. Brush with the remaining 1 tablespoon butter. Sprinkle with the remaining ¼ cup brown sugar, the cinnamon, and the remaining ¼ cup pecans. Starting at a wide end, roll up the dough jelly-roll style. With a sharp knife, cut into 9 equal slices and place cut side down in the baking dish. Bake for 18 to 20 minutes, or until puffed and golden. Remove from the oven and immediately invert onto a serving platter. **Be careful—the melted sugar is very hot.** Allow to cool slightly, then serve warm.

Chocolate-Banana Baked French Toast

4 TO 6 SERVINGS

The idea behind brunch is to serve dishes that are a little out of the ordinary and extra-special. This is the perfect example, 'cause it goes way beyond ordinary French toast. Why, the name speaks for itself . . . and so does the taste!

3 medium ripe bananas

4 eggs

¾ cup milk

¼ cup (½ stick) butter, melted

4 tablespoons sugar, divided

1 teaspoon vanilla extract

1 loaf (12 ounces) French bread, cut into 1-inch cubes

¼ cup miniature semisweet chocolate chips

Preheat the oven to 400°F. Coat a 9" × 13" baking dish with nonstick cooking spray. In a large bowl, mash the bananas with a fork. Add the eggs, milk, melted butter, 3 tablespoons sugar, and the vanilla; mix until well beaten. Add the bread and toss until completely coated. Pour into the baking dish and sprinkle with the chocolate chips and the remaining 1 table-spoon sugar. Bake for 18 to 20 minutes, or until set and golden. Cut into squares and serve.

> **TO KEEP THINGS EXCITING . . .**
> And sinful, top it with sliced bananas and ooey, gooey hot fudge. Mmm, mmm!

Baked Chocolate Chip Pancakes

12 TO 16 PANCAKE WEDGES

2¼ cups pancake and waffle mix

1½ cups milk

2 eggs

3 tablespoons sugar

1 tablespoon vegetable oil

1 teaspoon ground cinnamon

1 cup (6 ounces) semisweet chocolate chips

Over the years, I've received many letters asking about pancakes. It seems the most common question is how to make enough for the whole family without feeling like you've become a short-order cook. Well, hang up those aprons, 'cause with this recipe we can just mix up two big pancakes that we pop into the oven. Now we can all sit down and dig in at the same time!

Preheat the oven to 425°F. Coat two 12-inch pizza pans with nonstick cooking spray. In a large bowl, whisk all the ingredients except the chocolate chips until smooth. Divide the batter equally between the pizza pans, spreading evenly. Sprinkle the chocolate chips evenly over the batter. Bake for 10 to 12 minutes, or until the pancakes are lightly browned on top. Cut into wedges and serve.

> **HELPFUL HINT:**
> If you don't have two pizza pans, you can use one 10" × 15" rimmed cookie sheet for all the batter instead.

Open-faced Strawberry Cheese Danish

Ever try to make Danish from scratch? Trust me, it's a pretty long process. That's why I created this easy open-faced version using buttermilk biscuits, cream cheese, and jam. Now we can enjoy fresh Danish straight from the oven, without spending hours in the kitchen. It sounds like a super plan to me!

16 DANISH

1 package (17.3 ounces) buttermilk biscuits (8 biscuits)

4 ounces cream cheese, softened

1 egg

2 tablespoons sugar

¼ cup strawberry preserves

Preheat the oven to 375°F. Coat 16 muffin cups with nonstick cooking spray. Halve each biscuit by gently pulling it apart. Place each biscuit half in a muffin cup and press against the bottom and sides of the cup to form a crust. In a medium bowl, beat the cream cheese, egg, and sugar until smooth. Spoon into the crusts and top evenly with the preserves. Bake for 10 to 12 minutes, or until the edges are golden. Allow to cool slightly, then serve warm.

SO MANY OPTIONS!
For a nutty cheese Danish, replace the strawberry preserves with ¼ cup chopped walnuts or pecans.

Shortcut Fresh OJ

**ABOUT 1 QUART;
4 TO 6 SERVINGS**

4 cups (1 quart) premade or
made-from-concentrate orange juice

2 large oranges, peeled and
sectioned

*Sometimes it's impossible
to find fresh orange juice in
the stores. And squeezing it
ourselves can be a real
hassle (and a big mess!).
Sure, it's worth it, but
when we're pressed for
time, we can make this
super timesaving version
that tastes pretty darned
close to the real thing.*

In a blender, blend the orange
juice and orange sections until
the sections are broken up and well
combined.

TO KEEP THINGS EXCITING . . .
Add a little champagne to each
adult's glass of orange juice,
making sparkling mimosas.

Lunch
Soups, Salads, and Sandwiches

Take a look at most of the cookbooks that offer quick-and-easy meals. They usually give a whole lot of recipes—for dinner fare only. So what are we supposed to do for lunch?! I know everybody gets trapped in a lunch rut every once in a while—you know, with the same old turkey or ham sandwiches and the same old tossed salads. We'd all like to know there's something new and exciting waiting in our lunch boxes every day, but, for most of us, that means a bunch of ingredients and lots of work.

Uh-uh! No more! I'm about to rescue you from boring lunches. Say good-bye to the "same-old, plain-old," and shout hello to the new, the exciting, and, most important, the easy-and-fast-as-can-be. We're about to enjoy a whole new lunch menu full of savory soups, crunchy tossed salads, yummy sandwiches, and lots of *"OOH IT'S SO GOOD!!®"*

Lunch
Soups, Salads, and Sandwiches

Steak 'n' Potato Soup   36

Franks 'n' Beans Soup   37

Chicken Burrito Soup   38

Tuna Melt Soup   39

Cheese Potato Soup   40

Chilled Shrimp Cocktail Soup   41

Grilled Pesto Chicken Salad   42

Taco Salad Pie   43

Chicken and Potato Salad   44

Quiche Lorraine Salad   45

Cobb Salad   46

Big Bowl Antipasto   47

Stacked Tomato Salad   48

Lunch Box Philly Pita   49

Hot Dog Reubens   50

Hawaiian Stuffed Pizza   51

Join-the-Club Tortilla   52

Smoked Turkey Sandwiches   53

Barbecue Chicken Sandwiches   54

Chicken Cordon Bleu Sandwiches   55

Chicken Quesadillas   56

Curried Chicken Calzones   57

Shrimp Salad Croissants   58

Oriental Salad Egg Rolls   59

Grilled PBM&Bs   60

Steak 'n' Potato Soup

This hearty soup combines the tastes of a classic steak dinner. It's packed with thin slices of steak, chunks of potatoes, and sautéed mushrooms. One spoonful and they'll be thanking you for a lunchtime winner.

2 tablespoons butter

One 8-ounce strip steak, well trimmed and thinly sliced

½ pound sliced fresh mushrooms

2 cans (10½ ounces each) condensed French onion soup

2½ cups water

1 package (24 ounces) frozen potato wedges, cut into bite-sized pieces

½ teaspoon black pepper

Melt the butter in a soup pot over high heat. Add the steak and mushrooms and cook for 5 to 6 minutes, or until the steak is no longer pink. Add the remaining ingredients; mix well. Bring to a boil; boil for 6 to 8 minutes, or until heated through.

MONEY-SAVING TIP:
Any type of beef can be sliced and used for this soup. I usually try to make this when I have leftover steak, 'cause that way it's almost like getting two meals for the price of one.

LUNCH

36

Franks 'n' Beans Soup

6 TO 8 SERVINGS

1 tablespoon butter

1 small onion, diced

3 cans (16 ounces each) baked beans, undrained

2 cups water

½ pound hot dogs, thinly sliced

¼ cup ketchup

1 tablespoon yellow mustard

½ small green bell pepper, diced (optional)

Looking for something new to fill up the kids' Thermoses? Sometimes that can be hard, 'cause we all know how fickle kids can be. But they're sure to love this soup that tastes just like the classic favorite. And you know what else? It has the mustard and ketchup already mixed in!

Melt the butter in a soup pot over high heat. Add the onion and sauté until golden, stirring frequently. Add the remaining ingredients except the green pepper; mix well and cook for 10 to 12 minutes, or until heated through, stirring occasionally. If desired, top each portion with diced green pepper just before serving.

HELPFUL HINT:
Depending on the type of baked beans you use, you may need to add additional water or cook this a little longer to get it to the perfect soup consistency.

Chicken Burrito Soup

Say adios to messy burritos whose ingredients fall all over our plates (and sometimes our laps, too). Now we can dig our spoons into a new kind of tasty burrito, 'cause this one's a soup!

10 TO 12 SERVINGS

4 cans (14½ ounces each) ready-to-use chicken broth

1 cup water

1 jar (16 ounces) salsa

1 pound boneless, skinless chicken breasts, cut into ½-inch chunks

½ cup sliced black olives

Four 6-inch flour tortillas, cut into 3" × ¼" strips

½ cup (2 ounces) finely shredded Cheddar cheese

In a soup pot, bring the chicken broth, water, and salsa to a boil over high heat. Add the chicken and cook for 4 to 6 minutes, or until no pink remains in the chicken. Stir in the olives and tortilla strips and cook for 2 to 3 minutes, or until heated through. Sprinkle each portion with cheese just before serving.

SO MANY OPTIONS!
This soup can be as mild or spicy as you like, depending on the type of salsa you use.

Tuna Melt Soup

6 TO 8 SERVINGS

2 cans (10¾ ounces each) condensed cream of celery soup

5 cups milk

2 cans (6 ounces each) tuna, drained and flaked

3 cups (12 ounces) shredded sharp Cheddar cheese, divided

½ teaspoon black pepper

Most of us are pros at doing more than one thing at a time, like eating lunch while working at the computer or watching TV. Well, no more messes, 'cause now we can enjoy the taste of an old-time favorite, tuna melt, spoonful after creamy spoonful. It's simple, so serve it up in a mug and enjoy. Just be careful not to drip on the keyboard or remote control!

In a soup pot, combine the soup, milk, and tuna over medium heat; mix well. Add 2½ cups cheese and the pepper; mix well. Cook for 8 to 10 minutes, or until heated through and the cheese is melted, stirring frequently. Just before serving, sprinkle each bowl with some of the remaining ½ cup cheese.

TO FANCY IT UP:
Serve the soup in bread bowls made by cutting a circle out of the center of kaiser rolls. Then cut the circles into crouton-sized pieces for topping the soup.

Cheese Potato Soup

Who wouldn't savor the taste of an extra-creamy, super-cheesy baked potato? Now we can enjoy that taste in this rich soup that's ready in under 10 minutes. You'll think you're eating a baked potato! How's that for a quick and tasty lunch?

4 cans (14½ ounces each) ready-to-use chicken broth

2 cups (1 pint) half-and-half

3 cups instant mashed potato flakes

4 cups (16 ounces) shredded sharp Cheddar cheese, divided

½ teaspoon black pepper

3 scallions, thinly sliced

In a large saucepan, combine the chicken broth, half-and-half, potato flakes, 3½ cups cheese, and the pepper; mix well. Bring to a boil over medium-high heat, stirring constantly. Cook for 2 to 3 minutes, or until thickened, stirring constantly. Sprinkle each serving with some of the scallions and the remaining ½ cup cheese. Serve immediately.

FOR A CHANGE OF PACE: Mix in real bacon bits to make this a bacon 'n' cheese potato soup.

TO FANCY IT UP:
Use finely shredded Cheddar cheese rather than the traditional style—it not only melts quicker, but it looks prettier sprinkled over the soup, too.

LUNCH

40

Chilled Shrimp Cocktail Soup

4 TO 6 SERVINGS

3 cups vegetable juice, chilled

1 jar (11 ounces) cocktail sauce

1 package (10 ounces) frozen cooked salad shrimp, thawed

1 medium tomato, diced

½ medium green bell pepper, diced

½ medium cucumber, diced

2 scallions, thinly sliced

Going out to lunch every day can get a little expensive, so why not brown-bag it a few times a week? And what better way to start than with a cold shrimp cocktail soup? It's perfect for those hot summer days when we crave something light and refreshing, but filling at the same time. Won't we be the talk of the lunchroom!

In a large bowl, combine all the ingredients; mix well. Serve immediately, or cover and chill until ready to serve.

SO MANY OPTIONS!
For added zing, mix in some hot pepper sauce or prepared white horseradish.

Grilled Pesto Chicken Salad

It used to be that pesto was considered a fancy-schmancy flavoring, but now pesto is one of the many sauces available in our super-markets. And when it's teamed with grilled chicken, colorful sautéed peppers, and fresh spinach, it's a quick lunchtime delight.

3 medium bell peppers (1 each red, yellow, and green), cut into thin strips

2 tablespoons olive oil, divided

1 pound boneless, skinless chicken breasts, cut into thin strips

½ teaspoon salt

½ teaspoon black pepper

½ cup prepared pesto sauce

½ cup mayonnaise

1 package (10 ounces) fresh spinach, trimmed and torn into bite-sized pieces

In a medium bowl, toss the bell pepper strips with 1 tablespoon oil; coat well. Pre-heat a large grill pan or skillet over high heat. Add the peppers and grill for 4 to 5 minutes, or until crisp-tender and just starting to brown, turning occasionally. Meanwhile, in the same bowl, toss the chicken strips with the remaining 1 tablespoon oil, the salt, and black pepper. Remove the bell peppers from the pan and set aside. Grill the chicken for 3 to 4 minutes per side, or until no pink remains. In a large bowl, combine the pesto sauce and mayonnaise; mix well. Add the spinach and toss to coat. Place on a serving platter and top with the grilled peppers and chicken. Serve immediately.

SO MANY OPTIONS:
To make this even easier, use prewashed baby spinach leaves.

Taco Salad Pie

4 TO 6 SERVINGS

2 cans (10½ ounces each)
no-bean chili

1 can (16 ounces) refried beans

1 package (1¼ ounces) dry taco
seasoning mix

3 cups crushed tortilla chips

2 cups (8 ounces) shredded
Mexican cheese blend

2 cups shredded lettuce

1 medium tomato, diced

*Serving this for lunch?
It should come with this
warning: "This pie will
bring great satisfaction
and may need to be
followed by a siesta.
Eat at your own risk!"*

In a medium saucepan, combine the chili, refried beans, and taco seasoning mix over medium heat, stirring until well mixed and heated through. Place the crushed tortilla chips in a 9-inch deep-dish pie plate. Spoon the chili mixture over the crushed tortilla chips and top with the cheese, lettuce, and tomato. Serve immediately.

SO MANY OPTIONS!
Add additional toppings such as sliced jalapeño peppers, black olives, chopped green chilies, diced avocado, and/or chopped scallions.

Chicken and Potato Salad

My friends at the Radish Council shared this recipe with me. Try it in place of regular potato salad at your next picnic or barbecue. It's the perfect go-along for traditional grilled favorites, and talk about fresh-tasting . . .

6 medium potatoes, peeled and cut into 1-inch chunks

2 tablespoons salt

1 pound fresh asparagus, trimmed and cut into 1-inch pieces

½ cup frozen green peas, thawed

2 packages (10 ounces each) refrigerated cooked, sliced chicken breast

10 radishes, sliced

1 cup ranch dressing

Place the potatoes and salt in a soup pot and add enough water to cover the potatoes. Bring to a boil over high heat and let boil for 2 minutes; add the asparagus and peas. Cook for 2 to 3 minutes, or until the potatoes are tender and the asparagus is crisp-tender; drain, rinse with cold water, and drain again. Place in a large bowl and add the chicken, radishes, and dressing; toss well. Serve warm, or cover and chill until ready to serve.

HELPFUL HINT:
I use packaged sliced precooked chicken, which is widely available now in various flavors and can be found in the refrigerated meat section of most supermarkets.

SO MANY OPTIONS!
Sometimes I use unpeeled red potatoes for a slightly different flavor. They add a little extra color, too.

LUNCH

44

Quiche Lorraine Salad

4 TO 6 SERVINGS

When the mercury is rising and we're looking for a cool lunchtime option, this twist on a French classic is just what we need.

1 package (10 ounces) fresh spinach, trimmed and torn into bite-sized pieces

2 cups (8 ounces) shredded Swiss cheese

1 container (3 ounces) real bacon bits

¾ cup Caesar salad dressing

In a large bowl, combine all the ingredients; toss until mixed and the spinach is well coated. Serve immediately.

TO FANCY IT UP:
Top with herb-flavored croutons just before serving.

Cobb Salad

I bet most people don't know that Cobb Salad was created at the Brown Derby restaurant in Los Angeles as a way of using leftovers. Who knew leftovers could be so glamorous? I'll share another secret with you: In this case, glamour does not equal lots of work!

4 TO 6 SERVINGS

1 medium
head iceberg lettuce,
cut into bite-sized pieces

1 package (10 ounces) refrigerated
cooked, sliced chicken breast
(see Hint, page 44)

1 container (3 ounces) real bacon bits

1 large tomato, coarsely chopped

1 avocado, peeled, pitted, and chopped

3 hard-boiled eggs, chopped (optional)

4 scallions, thinly sliced

1 package (4 ounces) crumbled
blue cheese

Arrange the lettuce on a large serving platter. Arrange the remaining ingredients in rows over the lettuce. Serve, or cover and chill until ready to serve.

GREAT GO-ALONG:
Drizzle with a creamy
salad dressing like ranch
or Thousand Island.

Big Bowl Antipasto

1 large head
iceberg lettuce,
coarsely chopped

One ½-inch-thick slice (about ½ pound)
deli turkey breast, cut into cubes

Two ½-inch-thick slices (about ½ pound
total) deli hard salami, cut into cubes

One ½-inch-thick slice (about ½ pound)
provolone cheese, cut into cubes

1 can (6 ounces) pitted black olives, drained

1 jar (7 ounces) roasted peppers, drained
and cut into ½-inch strips

1 pint cherry tomatoes

1 bottle (8 ounces)
Italian dressing

Some of us might be intimidated by the thought of making an antipasto platter, 'cause we think it takes lots of work and it has to be just so. Not this one! There's no layering or rolling needed. Just toss it all in a big bowl, give it a mix, and it's ready to serve.

In a large bowl, combine all the ingredients except the dressing; mix well. Add the dressing and toss until well coated. Serve immediately.

LUNCH

47

TO FANCY IT UP:
Top the salad with peperoncini
and freshly grated
Parmesan cheese.

Stacked Tomato Salad

We've got some ruby red tomatoes fresh from the vine, and we're looking for some creative ways to use them. Sure, we can pack 'em with tuna or chicken salad, but why not go with the layered look? It's the most refreshing and impressive-looking lunch around.

4 medium ripe tomatoes

1 package (4 ounces) mixed baby greens

1/4 cup balsamic vinaigrette dressing

1/4 cup crumbled blue cheese

Cut a thin slice from the bottom of each tomato so the tomato sits flat; discard the slices. Cut each tomato horizontally into 5 slices, keeping the slices together. In a small bowl, combine the remaining ingredients; toss well. Place the bottom tomato slices on a serving dish, then top equally with a quarter of the salad mixture. Repeat the layers three more times, ending with the top tomato slices. Serve immediately.

> **SO MANY OPTIONS!**
> Any combination of ingredients can work with tomatoes sliced and served this way. Another of my favorites is a mixture of baby spinach leaves, bacon bits, and ranch dressing.

Lunch Box Philly Pita

4 SANDWICHES

1 pound thinly sliced deli roast beef, coarsely chopped

1 cup (4 ounces) finely shredded sharp Cheddar cheese

1 container (2.8 ounces) French-fried onions

Four 6-inch pita breads, each cut in half

If I told you it was possible to make a Philly cheese steak sandwich hours in advance and wrap it up to be microwaved right before eating, you probably wouldn't believe it. Well, believe me—and give it a try!

In a large bowl, combine all the ingredients except the bread; mix well. Place an equal amount of the mixture in each pita half. Wrap each half in waxed paper, then heat and serve, or chill until ready to serve. When ready to serve, heat in the microwave until heated through and the cheese is melted.

HELPFUL HINT:
These can also be unwrapped and heated in a 350°F. oven on a baking sheet for a few minutes, but they make a perfect brown-bag lunch, since microwaves can now be found in most offices and lunchrooms. In minutes, you'll be enjoying a hot Philly cheese steak sandwich!

Hot Dog Reubens

This recipe came from a viewer who wrote to tell me he started making lunch one day and didn't have the corned beef he needed to make a traditional Reuben. He substituted hot dogs and—what do you know— the hot dog Reuben was born!

2 teaspoons butter
4 jumbo hot dogs (1 pound)
¼ cup Thousand Island dressing
4 hot dog rolls
1 can (8 ounces) sauerkraut, drained
½ cup (2 ounces) shredded Swiss cheese

Preheat the broiler. Melt the butter in a large skillet over medium heat. Add the hot dogs and cook for 5 to 7 minutes, or until browned on all sides.
Spread the dressing evenly over the inside of the hot dog rolls; place the hot dogs in the rolls. Top with the sauerkraut, then sprinkle with the cheese. Place on a baking sheet and broil for 2 to 3 minutes, or until the cheese is melted. Serve immediately.

GREAT GO-ALONG:
Serve these with the traditional Reuben go-alongs of coleslaw, potato salad, and pickles.

Hawaiian Stuffed Pizza

4 WEDGES

One 12-inch frozen cheese pizza, thawed and cut in half

One ¼-inch-thick slice (about ¼ pound) deli ham, diced

1 can (8 ounces) pineapple tidbits, drained

½ cup (2 ounces) shredded sharp Cheddar cheese

Shh! Nobody has to know this one starts with a pre-made frozen pizza. We simply spruce it up with some diced ham and a bit of pineapple. Then, when we get all the compliments, we can take all the credit... without telling them the freezer case gave us a head start.

Preheat the oven to 425°F. Place a large sheet of aluminum foil on a baking sheet. Place one pizza half cheese side up on the pan and sprinkle with the ham and pineapple. Top with the remaining pizza half cheese side down, pressing the pizza halves together. Fold and seal the aluminum foil over the pizza. Bake for 15 minutes, then uncover the pizza and sprinkle evenly with the cheese. Bake, uncovered, for 5 to 7 minutes, or until the cheese has melted and the pizza is heated through.

> **GREAT GO-ALONG:**
> For a real tropical lunch, serve with an icy piña colada—with or without alcohol.

Join-the-Club Tortilla

It's time for our traditional layered club sandwich to move over and make room for this spin-off version. Oh—there's no club membership needed for this one, either!

3 tablespoons mayonnaise
Three 10-inch flour tortillas
8 iceberg lettuce leaves
½ pound thinly sliced deli turkey breast
8 slices cooked bacon
½ pound thinly sliced deli ham
4 slices (3 ounces) American cheese
1 medium tomato, cut into 8 slices

LUNCH

52

Spread the mayonnaise evenly over one side of each tortilla. Place 4 lettuce leaves on one tortilla, then top with the turkey and bacon. Place another tortilla over the bacon. Top with the remaining 4 lettuce leaves, the ham, cheese, tomato, and the remaining tortilla, mayonnaise side down. Slice into 4 wedges and serve immediately.

HELPFUL HINTS:
For easier cutting, place a toothpick in each wedge before slicing. Precooked bacon is now available packaged and ready to use. Look for it in your supermarket.

Smoked Turkey Sandwiches

4 SANDWICHES

⅓ cup mayonnaise

3 tablespoons blueberry preserves

1 loaf (12 ounces) French bread,
    cut lengthwise in half

½ head leaf lettuce

1 pound thinly sliced deli smoked
    turkey breast

Not all turkey sandwiches are created equal! Here's one that tops the list 'cause it's stuffed with crispy leaf lettuce and a touch of blueberry preserves. It's a little different . . . and definitely not boring.

In a small bowl, combine the mayonnaise and preserves; mix well. Spread over both cut sides of the French bread. Layer the lettuce over the bottom half of the bread. Top with the turkey, then replace the top of the bread. Cut into 4 sandwiches and serve.

SO MANY OPTIONS!
Go ahead and use any flavor of fruit preserves you prefer; almost any one will work to create a unique flavor.

Barbecue Chicken Sandwiches

We sure love our barbecue, don't we? Here's how to get that long-cooked taste when you're short on time!

8 SANDWICHES

2 teaspoons vegetable oil

1 medium onion, coarsely chopped

1 medium green bell pepper, coarsely chopped

½ pound fresh mushrooms, sliced

1 can (10 ounces) chunk chicken, drained and flaked

2 cups barbecue sauce

8 hamburger buns, split

Preheat the broiler. Heat the oil in a large skillet over medium heat. Add the onion, bell pepper, and mushrooms and sauté until the vegetables are crisp-tender. Add the chicken and barbecue sauce and cook until the mixture is heated through, stirring frequently. Meanwhile, place the split buns on a baking sheet and lightly toast under the broiler. Top the bottom halves with the chicken mixture, then replace the tops and serve.

SO MANY OPTIONS!
Try topping the chicken mixture on each sandwich with a slice of cheese studded with jalapeño pepper and broiling for 1 to 2 minutes before serving.

Chicken Cordon Bleu Sandwiches

4 SANDWICHES

1 package (10½ ounces) frozen fully cooked breaded chicken breast patties, thawed

One ¼-inch-thick slice (about ¼ pound) deli ham, quartered

1 cup (4 ounces) shredded Swiss cheese

4 romaine lettuce leaves

4 hamburger buns, split

Instead of eating a plain old chicken breast sand-wich again, try adding a little taste of France to your plate. Yup, by adding ham and cheese to breaded chicken breasts, we've cre-ated a shortcut lunchtime recipe that's full of great taste.

Coat a large skillet with non-stick cooking spray. Add the chicken and cook for 2 minutes over medium-high heat. Turn the chicken over and top each with a slice of ham, then an equal amount of cheese. Reduce the heat to medium, cover, and cook for 5 to 7 minutes, or until heated through and the cheese is melted. Place a lettuce leaf on each hamburger bun and top with the chicken cordon bleu. Serve immediately.

> **TO KEEP THINGS EXCITING . . .**
> I like to spread a little Dijon-style mustard on the buns. It gives this just the right flavor kick.

Chicken Quesadillas

Add a little spice to lunchtime with a quesadilla. What a crispy, tasty way to brighten up your day!

4 QUESADILLAS

1 can (10 ounces) chunk chicken, drained and flaked

2 cups (8 ounces) shredded Mexican cheese blend

Eight 10-inch flour tortillas

2 teaspoons vegetable oil

In a large bowl, combine the chicken and shredded cheese; mix well. Sprinkle evenly over 4 tortillas and top with the remaining 4 tortillas, making sandwiches. In a large skillet, heat ½ teaspoon oil over medium heat. Place one tortilla sandwich in the skillet and cook for 3 to 4 minutes, or until the cheese is melted, turning halfway through the cooking. Remove to a covered platter and repeat with the remaining sandwiches. Cut each quesadilla into 4 wedges and serve.

TO FANCY IT UP:
After cutting each quesadilla, dollop the center with some sour cream, salsa, and a sprinkling of sliced scallions.

Curried Chicken Calzones

4 CALZONES

Put away the Parmesan cheese and crushed red pepper, 'cause this calzone is far from the traditional Italian tomato-and-cheese version. It's a quick toss-together lunch.

1 package (15 ounces) folded refrigerated pie crusts (2 crusts)

¾ pound ½-inch-thick deli chicken roll, cubed

1 can (15¼ ounces) tropical fruit salad, drained

¼ cup golden raisins

1 tablespoon cornstarch

2 teaspoons curry powder

¼ teaspoon black pepper

Nonstick cooking spray

Preheat the oven to 450°F. Coat two baking sheets with nonstick cooking spray. Unfold the pie crusts. Cut each in half and place on the baking sheets. In a medium bowl, combine the remaining ingredients; mix well. Spread an equal amount of the mixture over half of each crust half, leaving a ½-inch border. Fold the pie crust over the filling, forming triangles. With a fork, pinch the edges together firmly to seal. Coat the tops of the calzones with nonstick cooking spray. Bake for 12 to 14 minutes, or until the crust is golden. Serve immediately.

LUNCH

57

TIMESAVING TIP:
Arrange your spices alphabetically so you can always find what you need in a jiffy.

Shrimp Salad Croissants

We all deserve a little pampering once in a while. I can't think of any better way to do that than to sink your teeth into a large croissant stuffed with chunky shrimp salad. Go ahead, live a little!

1 package (10 ounces) frozen cooked salad shrimp, thawed

3 ribs celery, finely chopped

½ cup mayonnaise

¼ teaspoon black pepper

4 large croissants, sliced horizontally in half

In a large bowl, combine all the ingredients except the croissants; mix well. Spread equal amounts of the shrimp salad over the bottom halves of the croissants, then replace the tops and serve.

LUNCH

58

SO MANY OPTIONS!
For variety, why not add chopped pecans or green grapes to this salad?

Oriental Salad Egg Rolls

8 EGG ROLLS

1 package (10 ounces) Oriental complete bagged salad kit

2 tablespoons mayonnaise

1 can (6 ounces) tiny cocktail shrimp, drained

8 egg roll wrappers

2 teaspoons vegetable oil

Hmm, a bunch of crunchy Oriental veggies mixed with creamy dressing and baked inside a crispy shell? It sure sounds like a recipe for success!

Preheat the oven to 450°F. Coat a baking sheet with nonstick cooking spray. In a large bowl, combine the package of Oriental dressing and the mayonnaise until smooth. Coarsely chop the mixed greens and vegetables from the salad kit and add to the dressing mixture. Add the noodles from the kit and the shrimp; mix well. Spoon an equal amount of the mixture onto the center of each egg roll wrapper. Fold one corner of each wrapper over the salad mixture, then fold the two sides over envelope fashion. Roll the egg roll over toward the remaining corner to close and place seam side down on the baking sheet. Brush each egg roll with oil and bake for 12 to 14 minutes, or until golden and crisp. Serve immediately.

LUNCH

59

> **HELPFUL HINT:**
> Oriental bagged salad kits, containing mixed greens and vegetables, packaged dressing, and crispy noodles, can usually be found with the other bagged salads in the produce department of your supermarket.

Grilled *PBM&Bs*

Peanut butter teams well with so many flavors, especially chocolate and marshmallow creme. Believe it or not, a recent survey added bananas to the list, too. So dig into this yummy sandwich that's really quite "a-peeling."

4 SANDWICHES

¼ cup creamy peanut butter
8 slices cinnamon-raisin bread
⅓ cup marshmallow creme
2 large bananas, peeled
2 tablespoons butter

Spread equal amounts of peanut butter over 4 slices of bread. Spread equal amounts of marshmallow creme over the remaining 4 slices of bread. Cut the bananas crosswise, in half, then slice each half lengthwise into 3 slices. Place 3 slices of banana over the peanut butter on each slice of bread, then top with the remaining bread, marshmallow creme side down. In a large skillet or griddle, melt 1 tablespoon butter over medium-low heat. Place two sandwiches in the skillet; cook for 2 minutes, then turn the sandwiches over and cook for 1 to 2 more minutes, or until golden. Repeat with the remaining 1 tablespoon butter and sandwiches. Serve immediately.

SO MANY OPTIONS!
Sure, you can use any kind of bread—white, wheat, or, my favorite for this recipe, egg bread (challah).

Snack Attack

When kids hear the word *snack*, they probably think of the big plates of cookies and glasses of milk that are the usual after-school hunger-busters. But we adults have lots of other types of snacks that we eat during the day. That bag of pretzels we keep in our desk drawer at the office is one. So is the plate of goodies we munch on when doing projects or watching our evening TV. See—we really eat snacks a lot more than we think. Most of us just love to munch!

The next time the munchies hit, instead of reaching for a bag of chips or heating up another frozen pizza, why not try one of these new treats? You can eat 'em at home, at the office, after school . . . why, most of them can be enjoyed anywhere and anytime. And they're as easy as cookies and milk—but lots more exciting!

Snack Attack

Easy Arepas   64

Peanut Butter Cup Roll-ups   65

Sweet-and-Salty Cookies   66

Carrot Cake Cookies   67

Cheesy Apple Cider Fondue   68

Cinnamon-Sugar Pretzels   69

Fruit Roll Sushi   70

Super-Smooth Smoothie   71

Peanut Butter–Chocolate Candy   72

Chocolate Peanut Butter Pretzels   73

Chocolate Chip Ice Cream Sandwiches   74

Awesome Freezer S'mores   75

Pizza Crisps   76

Cheesy Beer Dip   77

Hot Dog Puffs   78

Bacon 'n' Cheese Bites   79

Bite-Sized Mexican Pizzas   80

Barbecue Blue Chips   81

Buffalo Chicken Tenders   82

Piled-High Nachos   83

Artichoke-Crab Pizza Wedges   84

Pesto Chicken Bruschetta   85

White Pita Pizza   86

Cinnamon-Toast Popcorn   87

Easy Arepas

What's an arepa? It's a small round ground-corn cake that's either pan- or deep-fried. This South American dish is often filled with cheese, as I've done here in this yummy simplified version.

1 tablespoon butter

6 slices (4½ ounces) Mexican-flavored American cheese

1 package (7½ ounces) frozen corn toaster muffins (6 muffins), thawed

Melt the butter in a large skillet over medium-low heat. Place 2 slices of cheese on the flat side of each of 3 toaster muffins. Top each with another toaster muffin and place in the skillet. Cover and cook for 3 to 4 minutes per side, or until golden and the cheese is melted. Serve immediately.

SNACK ATTACK

64

HELPFUL HINT:
Corn toaster muffins can be found either near the baked goods or in the frozen food section of your supermarket, next to the frozen waffles and pancakes.

Peanut Butter Cup Roll-ups

¾ cup creamy peanut butter

Four 10-inch flour tortillas

½ cup miniature semisweet chocolate chips

The kids are home from school and just begging for a snack, but you're sure you're all out. Oh yeah? Betcha you've got some peanut butter and chocolate chips in the cupboard, and even some tortillas in the fridge or freezer. That's all you need to throw together these roll-ups. Then all you'll hear is lots of lip smacking and requests for more!

Spread the peanut butter over the tortillas, then sprinkle evenly with the chocolate chips. Roll up tightly jelly-roll style. Wrap each in a sheet of waxed paper, twisting the ends to seal. Microwave for 10 to 15 seconds, or until the chocolate chips are melted. Serve immediately.

SNACK ATTACK

65

TIMESAVING TIP:
This is the perfect snack to prepare ahead of time and keep chilled. Then anytime you need a quick pick-me-up, just microwave one until warmed through and the chips have melted.

Sweet-and-Salty Cookies

For some reason, we often crave the taste of snacks that are at the same time both sweet and salty, so here's a combination of sugar cookies and pretzels that your taste buds will fall in love with.

ABOUT 2 DOZEN COOKIES

1 package (18 ounces) refrigerated sugar cookie dough

1 cup coarsely crushed pretzels

Preheat the oven to 350°F. Shape the cookie dough into 1-inch balls. Place the crushed pretzels in a shallow dish. Roll the balls in the pretzels, coating completely. Place 1 inch apart on ungreased cookie sheets and bake for 12 to 14 minutes, or until golden.

TO KEEP THINGS EXCITING . . .
Use crushed chocolate-covered pretzels, widely available in supermarkets, instead of plain pretzels.

Carrot Cake Cookies

ABOUT 5 DOZEN COOKIES

1 package (18 ounces)
carrot cake mix

1 can (8 ounces) crushed
pineapple, drained

2 carrots, finely shredded

2 eggs

2 tablespoons vegetable oil

1 cup chopped pecans

It's pretty hard to find after-school snacks that not only taste good but are nutritious, too. Well, here's a way to sneak healthy veggies into snack time. These cookies taste so incredible, nobody will believe they're packed with goodness . . . so don't tell them till after the cookies are gone!

Preheat the oven to 350°F. Coat cookie sheets with nonstick cooking spray. In a large bowl, combine the cake mix, pineapple, carrots, eggs, and oil; beat for 3 to 4 minutes, or until well blended. Stir in the pecans. Drop by teaspoonfuls 1 inch apart onto the cookie sheets. Bake for 14 to 16 minutes, or until the edges are golden. Remove to a wire rack to cool. Serve warm, or allow to cool completely before serving.

SO MANY OPTIONS!
The usual bonus with carrot cake is the cream cheese frosting, so you may want to frost these with prepared (or homemade) cream cheese frosting.

Cheesy Apple Cider Fondue

That's right—the fondue we all loved years ago is making a comeback at tables everywhere. It makes sense, since fondue's so easy to make, and it works for mealtime, snack time, and whenever! Come on and give it a try—you just heat a few ingredients, then dunk to your heart's content.

¾ cup apple cider

2 cups (8 ounces) finely shredded Cheddar cheese

1 cup (4 ounces) shredded Swiss cheese

1 tablespoon cornstarch

¼ teaspoon salt

⅛ teaspoon black pepper

In a medium saucepan, heat the apple cider over medium heat until bubbly. Meanwhile, in a medium bowl, combine the remaining ingredients; mix well. Add the cheese mixture to the cider a little at a time and stir continuously for 4 to 5 minutes, or until the mixture is thoroughly blended and smooth. Transfer to a fondue pot or place the saucepan on a warming tray to keep the fondue hot. Serve immediately.

GREAT GO-ALONG:
Serve with apple and pear wedges and chunks of crusty bread for dunking.

Cinnamon-Sugar Pretzels

8 PRETZELS

1 package (11 ounces) refrigerated soft bread stick dough

¼ cup sugar

¼ teaspoon ground cinnamon

2 tablespoons butter, melted

Why settle for plain old pretzels when it's just as easy to enjoy fresh piping-hot ones coated with cinnamon and sugar? Yup, they're a sweet "twist" on the old favorites.

Preheat the oven to 375°F. Coat a baking sheet with nonstick cooking spray. Unroll the bread sticks and separate into 8 strips. Form each strip into a pretzel shape and place on the baking sheet. In a small bowl, combine the sugar and cinnamon. Brush the pretzels with the melted butter, then sprinkle with the sugar-cinnamon mixture. Bake for 13 to 15 minutes, or until golden. Serve immediately.

TO KEEP THINGS EXCITING . . . Sometimes I like to melt extra butter and mix in a little sugar and cinnamon to make a dipping sauce for the pretzels.

Fruit Roll Sushi

SNACK ATTACK

When you tell the kids you're serving sushi as an after-school snack, there are sure to be cries of "Ooh, that's gross! I'm not trying that!" But once they hear it's fruit roll sushi, made with all the things they love, the cries will change to "Yummy!" and "More, please!"

ABOUT 2 1/2 DOZEN PIECES

1 tablespoon butter

12 marshmallows

2 cups Rice Krispies cereal

Four 4 1/2-inch square fruit roll-ups (1/2 ounce each)

6 assorted licorice or fruit twist sticks, cut crosswise in half

Melt the butter in a medium saucepan over low heat. Add the marshmallows and stir until completely melted. Remove from the heat and stir in the cereal until completely coated. On a flat surface, unroll the fruit roll-ups. Spread an equal amount of the cereal mixture over each roll-up, covering the entire surface and packing the mixture flat. Place 3 different-colored licorice or fruit twists across the center of each and roll tightly into a log; press to seal the seam where the edges meet. Squeeze the rolls gently to secure. Trim the ends and slice with a serrated knife into 1/2-inch pieces. Serve, or store in an airtight container until ready to serve.

TO KEEP THINGS EXCITING . . .
Make sure to use different colored/flavored fruit roll-ups and licorice or fruit twist sticks.

Super-Smooth Smoothie

2 TO 3 SERVINGS

½ cup milk

1 container (8 ounces) vanilla yogurt

2 tablespoons honey

2 cups frozen peach slices

Smoothies are a super-healthy snack 'cause they're packed with lots of good-for-you fruit. Ready in minutes, they're a perfect take-along snack.

Place all the ingredients in a blender in the order listed; blend until smooth. Serve immediately.

FOR A CHANGE OF PACE:
Use a different fruit for a whole new taste sensation. Try frozen strawberries, blueberries, raspberries, or another favorite fruit. The possibilities are endless!

Peanut Butter–Chocolate Candy

There are very few things that will satisfy a snack attack better than plain chocolate. But I've got one. It's a creamy combination of chocolate and peanut butter—and it's a winner every time.

4 cups confectioners' sugar

1 cup creamy peanut butter

1 cup (2 sticks) butter, melted

1 cup graham cracker crumbs

2 cups (12 ounces) semisweet chocolate chips, melted

Coat a 10" × 15" rimmed baking sheet with nonstick cooking spray. In a large bowl, mix all the ingredients except the chocolate until well combined. Spread over the bottom of the baking sheet. Spread the melted chocolate evenly over the peanut butter layer. Freeze for 15 minutes, then cut into squares. Serve, or cover and keep refrigerated until ready to serve.

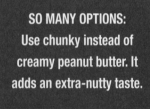

SO MANY OPTIONS:
Use chunky instead of creamy peanut butter. It adds an extra-nutty taste.

Chocolate Peanut Butter Pretzels

1 DOZEN PRETZELS

If chocolate-covered pretzels are high on your family's snack list, imagine how much higher they're going to be with the added taste of peanut butter. Why, they'll be a 10+!

Twelve 3-inch pretzels
⅓ cup milk chocolate chips
¼ cup chunky peanut butter

Line a baking sheet with waxed paper. Place the pretzels on the baking sheet. In a small saucepan, melt the chocolate chips and peanut butter over low heat, stirring occasionally, until smooth. Use a fork to drizzle the mixture over the pretzels. Chill for 15 minutes, or until the chocolate is firm. Serve, or cover and keep chilled until ready to serve.

SO MANY OPTIONS!
Would you rather skip the peanut butter flavor? Just drizzle the pretzels with plain chocolate or maybe white or semisweet chocolate.

Chocolate Chip Ice Cream Sandwiches

Forget those boring ice cream sandwiches that you get in a box. Let's face it. Given the choice between those and creamy ice cream slathered between fresh chocolate chip cookies and rolled in chocolate chips, which would you choose? I thought you'd see my point!

1 package (18 ounces) refrigerated chocolate chip cookie dough

1 cup (6 ounces) miniature semisweet chocolate chips

1 quart chocolate chip ice cream

Preheat the oven to 350°F. Using a sharp knife, cut the cookie dough into 24 slices, and bake according to the package directions. Remove the cookies to a wire rack to cool. Place the chocolate chips on a plate. Allow the ice cream to soften slightly, then place 1 small scoop on the flat side of a cookie; place another cookie flat side down on the ice cream. Squeeze the 2 cookies together until the ice cream is pushed to the edges. Roll the edges of the sandwich over the chocolate chips until chips stick to the ice cream. Lightly press the chips into the ice cream and place the sandwich on a cookie sheet. Place in the freezer. Continue with the remaining cookies, ice cream, and chips. Serve, or wrap individually in plastic wrap and keep frozen until ready to serve.

FOR A CHANGE OF PACE:
Substitute 1/2 cup of your favorite chopped nuts for the chocolate chips.

SNACK ATTACK

74

Awesome Freezer S'mores

1 package (16 ounces)
graham crackers

1 jar (7 ounces) marshmallow creme

One ½-gallon block
chocolate ice cream

In the past, the only time most of us ate s'mores was sitting around a roaring campfire or maybe at a backyard barbecue. Not anymore! Here's an easy way to make s'mores right in our kitchens. And there are no messy ashes to clean up this time . . . just sticky fingers!

Place the graham crackers on a flat surface. Spread the marshmallow creme over one side of each graham cracker. Remove the ice cream from the container and slice crosswise into 8 equal slices. Cut each slice in half lengthwise and place each over a marshmallow-creme-topped graham cracker. Top each with a second graham cracker, marshmallow-creme side down. Press firmly together to form sandwiches and serve, or wrap individually and freeze until ready to serve.

SNACK ATTACK

75

TO KEEP THINGS EXCITING . . .
Get s'more of a good thing by using rocky road or chocolate chocolate chip ice cream instead of plain chocolate.

Pizza Crisps

These savory chips are perfect for having on hand to satisfy the munchies, whether you're at work, at home, or on the go.

½ cup (1 stick) butter, melted

1 package (1¼ ounces) dry spaghetti sauce mix

Ten 8-inch flour tortillas

¼ cup grated Parmesan cheese

Preheat the oven to 375°F. In a small bowl, combine the butter and spaghetti sauce mix; mix well. Spread evenly over one side of the tortillas, then sprinkle with the Parmesan cheese. Cut each tortilla into 8 wedges and place on baking sheets. Bake for 8 to 10 minutes, or until the chips are golden and crispy.

GREAT GO-ALONG:
Have some marinara sauce warmed up and ready for dunking!

Cheesy Beer Dip

ABOUT 1 ¼ CUPS

This one's for adults only, so mix up a batch, put your feet up, and relax. We all deserve a little quiet time, and there's no better way to enjoy it than with this spicy dip.

2 cups (8 ounces) shredded Mexican cheese blend

½ cup thick-and-chunky salsa

¼ cup beer

In a small saucepan, combine all the ingredients and cook over medium heat for 3 to 5 minutes, or until smooth and the cheese is melted, stirring frequently. Serve immediately.

SO MANY OPTIONS!
There are many different types of Mexican cheese blends available—some are spicier than others. So depending on the spiciness of the cheese and the type of salsa you use, this can be as spicy or as mild as you like. Regular, light, or even nonalcoholic beer can be used, but make sure to have plenty of tortilla chips on hand for dipping.

Hot Dog Puffs

Instead of making plain old pigs in blankets again, let's try something a little different. Start by wrapping hot dogs in biscuit dough, but this time spread the mustard and relish right on the dough before baking. Then we won't even have to dunk the finished puffs—we can just pop them right in our mouths!

1 package (7½ ounces) refrigerated biscuits (10 biscuits)
1 tablespoon yellow mustard
1 tablespoon pickle relish, drained
10 cocktail franks

Preheat the oven to 450°F. Coat a baking sheet with non-stick cooking spray. Separate the biscuits and flatten each with the palm of your hand. Spread the mustard and relish evenly over each biscuit. Place 1 cocktail frank at one edge of each biscuit and roll up. Cut each in half and place seam side down on the baking sheet. Bake for 7 to 9 minutes, or until the biscuits are golden. Serve immediately.

> **GREAT GO-ALONG:**
> There's already mustard inside, but if you want, go ahead and serve these with spicy mustard to give them extra zip.

Bacon 'n' Cheese Bites

ABOUT 2 DOZEN PIECES

Want something to make ahead and keep in the freezer for drop-in guests? Here you go!

1 cup biscuit baking mix

½ cup process cheese spread

½ cup (2 ounces) finely shredded
Cheddar cheese

2 tablespoons real bacon bits

⅓ cup club soda

Preheat the oven to 450°F. Coat two rimmed baking sheets with nonstick cooking spray. In a medium bowl, beat all the ingredients except the club soda until well mixed. Add the club soda and beat until well combined. Let stand for 5 minutes. Drop by teaspoonfuls 2 inches apart onto the baking sheets. Bake for 7 to 10 minutes, or until golden. Serve immediately.

FOR A CHANGE OF PACE:
Replace the club soda with beer. It'll give these even richer flavor.

Bite-Sized Mexican Pizzas

Uh-oh, you've got a snack attack that just won't go away! These mini pizzas are just the cure. And, lucky for us, they taste much better than medicine!

24 Triscuit® crackers

½ cup thick-and-chunky salsa

1 can (2¼ ounces) sliced black olives, drained (optional)

½ cup (2 ounces) shredded Mexican cheese blend

Preheat the oven to 450°F. Coat a baking sheet with nonstick cooking spray. Arrange the crackers on the baking sheet. Spoon the salsa evenly over the crackers. Top with the olives, if desired, and sprinkle with the cheese. Bake for 4 to 6 minutes, or until heated through and the cheese is melted. Serve immediately.

SNACK ATTACK

80

TO KEEP THINGS EXCITING . . .
And spicy, add a few sliced jalapeño peppers.

Barbecue Blue Chips

4 TO 6 SERVINGS

These may go together just like nachos, but they taste like everybody's favorite Buffalo-style chicken wings.

1 package (7½ ounces) ridged barbecue-flavored potato chips

1 can (5 ounces) chunk chicken, drained and flaked

1 package (4 ounces) crumbled blue cheese

Preheat the oven to 425°F. Place the chips on a large rimmed baking sheet. Sprinkle evenly with the chicken, then the blue cheese and bake for 4 to 5 minutes, or until heated through and the cheese is melted. Serve immediately.

TO FANCY IT UP:
Top with sliced scallions or, for a bit of spiciness, some sliced jalapeño peppers just before serving.

Buffalo Chicken Tenders

With our busy schedules, it's not too often that the entire family spends an evening together. So when it does happen, we want to make the night extra-special. We can start by renting a comedy or an action-packed video. Then we prepare a few snacks, making sure to put Buffalo chicken tenders on the top of the list, 'cause, after all, they're guaranteed to earn two thumbs up from your panel of critics!

½ cup all-purpose flour

½ cup hot cayenne pepper sauce (see Hint)

1 cup plain bread crumbs

1 pound boneless, skinless chicken breast halves, cut into 1-inch strips

Nonstick cooking spray

Preheat the oven to 425°F. Coat a baking sheet with nonstick cooking spray. Place the flour, hot sauce, and bread crumbs in three separate shallow dishes. Dip the chicken strips in the flour, then the hot sauce, then the bread crumbs, coating evenly with each, and place the coated strips on the baking sheet. Coat the chicken with nonstick cooking spray and bake for 8 minutes. Turn the chicken over, coat with nonstick cooking spray, and cook for 2 to 3 more minutes, or until the chicken is cooked through and the breading is golden brown. Serve immediately.

HELPFUL HINT:
Make sure to use hot *cayenne* pepper sauce, not simply hot pepper sauce ... unless you like your chicken *really hot*. And don't forget the traditional Buffalo wing go-alongs—celery sticks and blue cheese dressing.

Piled-High Nachos

8 TO 10 SERVINGS

2 cans
(15 ounces each) chili
with beans

1 package (1¼ ounces) dry taco
seasoning mix

1 package (14½ ounces) tortilla chips

2 cups (8 ounces) shredded Mexican
cheese blend

½ cup sour cream

1 tomato, diced

2 scallions, thinly sliced

½ cup prepared guacamole
(optional)

No snack collection is complete without a recipe for nachos. And since they're a favorite of snack lovers everywhere, get ready to hit new heights when you finish piling it on!

Preheat the oven to 425°F. In a medium bowl, combine the chili and taco seasoning mix; mix well. Spread the tortilla chips over two large rimmed baking sheets. Spoon the chili mixture evenly over the chips and sprinkle with the cheese. Bake for 5 to 7 minutes, or until heated through and the cheese is melted. Top with the sour cream, tomato, scallions, and guacamole, if desired. Serve immediately.

TO LIGHTEN IT UP:
Use reduced-fat sour cream and shredded cheese blend—those should do the trick.

Artichoke-Crab Pizza Wedges

Instead of serving plain old cheese pizza squares again, how about a new and exciting pizza? Yup, the creamy combination of artichokes and crabmeat gives us a taste we love without a lot of work.

16 WEDGES

⅔ cup mayonnaise

1 can (14 ounces) artichoke hearts, drained and chopped

1 can (6 ounces) crabmeat, drained and flaked

1 jar (2 ounces) chopped pimientos, drained

1 cup (4 ounces) *shredded* Parmesan cheese

6 scallions, thinly sliced

1½ teaspoons grated orange peel (optional)

One 12-inch prepared pizza shell

Preheat the oven to 450°F. In a medium bowl, combine all the ingredients except the pizza shell; mix well. Place the pizza shell on a pizza pan. Spread the crab mixture evenly over the top. Bake for 18 to 20 minutes, or until the topping is puffed and golden and the crust is brown and crisp. Cut into 16 thin wedges and serve.

SNACK ATTACK

84

MONEY-SAVING TIP:
Substitute imitation crabmeat for the real thing. It's a lot less expensive and works just fine.

Pesto Chicken Bruschetta

ABOUT 2 DOZEN SLICES

½ cup prepared pesto sauce

One loaf (12 ounces) French bread, cut into ½-inch slices (about 2 dozen)

1 package (10 ounces) refrigerated cooked, sliced chicken breast (see Hint, page 44)

¾ cup (3 ounces) shredded mozzarella cheese

When we have a serious case of the munchies and need something on the hearty side, we'll be giving three cheers for bruschetta. It's warm and satisfying, and it really takes the edge off.

Preheat the oven to 375°F. Spread the pesto sauce over each bread slice. Top with the chicken and sprinkle with the cheese. Place on baking sheets and bake for 8 to 10 minutes, or until heated through and the cheese is melted.

TO FANCY IT UP:
Add color and flavor by topping this with a few chopped plum tomatoes and maybe some chopped fresh basil before sprinkling with the cheese and baking.

White Pita Pizza

We're watching TV and our stomachs start to grumble. All we have to do is wait for the commercial to start, stroll into the kitchen, and whip up these pita pizzas. They're so quick that they'll be ready before the next commercial break!

Six 6-inch pita breads
¾ cup Alfredo sauce
⅓ cup shredded mozzarella cheese
⅓ cup *shredded* Parmesan cheese
2 tablespoons finely chopped fresh parsley

Preheat the oven to 450°F. Coat two large baking sheets with non-stick cooking spray. Place the pita bread on the baking sheets and top evenly with the Alfredo sauce. In a small bowl, combine the remaining ingredients; mix well and sprinkle over the Alfredo sauce. Bake for 7 to 10 minutes, or until heated through and the edges are golden. Cut into wedges and serve.

HELPFUL HINT:
Use shredded Parmesan cheese, not the grated type that we get in a can. Besides looking better, shredded Parmesan has more body.

Cinnamon-Toast Popcorn

ABOUT 8 CUPS

Plain popcorn is tasty, but your gang will be popping out of their seats for more of this sweet-and-sassy kind.

8 cups popped popcorn
2 tablespoons butter, melted
3 tablespoons confectioners' sugar
½ teaspoon ground cinnamon

Preheat the oven to 350°F. Coat a large rimmed baking sheet with nonstick cooking spray. Place the popcorn in a resealable plastic storage bag. In a small bowl, combine the butter and sugar; mix well and add to the popcorn. Add the cinnamon, seal the bag, and shake until the popcorn is well coated. Spread it over the baking sheet. Bake for 10 minutes, stirring after 5 minutes. Serve warm, or allow to cool completely and store in an airtight container until ready to serve.

HELPFUL HINT:
One regular package of microwaveable popcorn will yield 7 to 8 cups of popcorn, so you can use any plain (unflavored) variety for this.

Family Dinner

Carpools, voice mail, laundry, appointments, housecleaning, paperwork, e-mail . . . it's a wonder we can even think straight, much less get a balanced dinner on the table every night! With today's hectic lifestyles, there's just so much to do in so little time. And it seems like these days so many people are neglecting the really important things—like spending quality time with our families—in favor of doing chores like unloading and reloading the dishwasher. Of course that's not how we prefer to spend our precious time, but often we have no choice. And that means we need all the kitchen help we can get.

Well, here it is! Dinnertime doesn't have to mean busy time, 'cause I've created a whole bunch of new dinner recipes that are my easiest yet. Why, in under 30 minutes we can have a complete meal on the table—yes, including cooking time! And you know what that means? We can spend more time with our families and get back to what's most important.

Family Dinner

Stovetop Meat Loaves   93

Roast Beef "Crepes"   94

Quick-as-a-Wink Beef Stew   95

Orange Beef Teriyaki   96

Country-French Patties   97

Cheeseburger Bake   98

Beat-the-Clock Goulash   99

Ravioli Cacciatore   100

Smothered Pork Chops   101

Twenty-Minute Italian Chili   102

Marmalade Dijon Pork Chops   103

Country Barbecue Ribs   104

Fancy Fast Greek Chicken   105

Polynesian Chicken   106

Chicken Vegetable Penne   107

Crispy Fish 'n' Chips   108

Gobble-It-Up Spaghetti   109

Parmesan Turkey Meat Loaves   110

Skillet Chicken Noodle Parmigiana   111

Creamy Crab Casserole   112

Fish Parmigiana   113

Shrimp "Fried" Rice   114

Stovetop Tuna Casserole   115

Clams Scampi   116

Spinach Pasta Soufflé   117

One-Pot Macaroni and Cheese   118

Vegetable Couscous   119

Stovetop Meat Loaves

4 SERVINGS

1 pound ground beef

½ cup stuffing mix

1 small onion, finely chopped

1 egg

1 can (11⅛ ounces) condensed Italian tomato soup, divided

¼ teaspoon salt

1 tablespoon vegetable oil

¼ cup water

Meat loaf is still one of the ultimate comfort foods. What isn't comforting is how long it traditionally takes to bake a whole meat loaf. Well, guess what— these mini loaves capture that old-fashioned taste in less than half the time!

In a large bowl, combine the ground beef, stuffing mix, onion, egg, ¼ cup soup, and the salt; mix well. Shape the beef mixture into 4 mini loaves about ½ inch thick. Heat the oil in a large skillet over medium heat. Add the meat loaves and brown on both sides; drain off any fat. Stir the water into the remaining soup and pour over the meat loaves. Reduce the heat to medium-low, cover, and cook for 15 to 20 minutes, or until no pink remains in the meat, stirring the sauce occasionally. Serve topped with the sauce.

GREAT GO-ALONG:
While the meat loaves are cooking, we can whip up a batch of instant mashed potatoes and microwave a package of frozen peas.

Roast Beef "Crepes"

Why settle for cold sandwiches again when we can use deli roast beef to make these tasty roll-ups? They're just mashed potatoes and mixed veggies wrapped in a tasty piece of roast beef and topped with gravy. Sounds pretty comforting (and hassle-free), doesn't it?

2 cups warm prepared mashed potatoes

1 can (15 ounces) mixed vegetables, drained

8 thick slices deli roast beef (about 1¼ pounds)

1 jar (12 ounces) beef gravy

½ cup water

In a medium bowl, combine the mashed potatoes and mixed vegetables; mix well. Place an equal amount of the mixture at one end of each roast beef slice; roll up crepe-style. In a large deep skillet, combine the gravy and water over medium heat until bubbly. Add the beef rolls seam side down, cover, and simmer for 10 to 15 minutes, or until heated through. Serve with the gravy spooned over the top of the rolls.

GREAT GO-ALONG:
This is already an all-in-one meal, but you might want to start dinner with a Caesar salad and some warm rolls to fill it out.

Quick-as-a-Wink Beef Stew

2 jars
(12 ounces each) beef gravy

1½ cups water

Three ½-inch-thick slices (about
1½ pounds) deli roast beef, cubed

2 cans (14½ ounces each) whole
new potatoes, drained (with any large
potatoes quartered)

1 package (16 ounces) frozen
pearl onions, thawed

½ teaspoon black pepper

2 cans (14½ ounces each)
sliced carrots, drained

It used to be that cooking beef stew was a long, drawn-out process. It took hours to slice and brown the beef, chop the veggies, and cook it all. Haven't you wished for an easier version that still has old-time homemade slow-cooked taste? Your wish is granted . . . and it's ready quick as a wink, just like the name says.

In a soup pot, combine all the ingredients except the carrots over high heat. Bring to a boil and cook for 6 to 8 minutes, or until heated through, stirring frequently. Add the carrots, stirring until warmed through. Serve.

HELPFUL HINT:
When buying the roast beef from the deli, just ask that it be cut into ½-inch-thick slices; then you just have to cut it into cubes.

TIMESAVING TIP:
Freeze individual portions of leftover dinners in microwaveable containers for quick ready-in-minutes meals.

FAMILY DINNER

95

Orange Beef Teriyaki

How can something so quick be so good? In just 15 short minutes, you'll have the answer!

4 TO 6 SERVINGS

2 tablespoons vegetable oil

1½ pounds beef stir-fry meat

1 can (11 ounces) mandarin oranges, drained, with liquid reserved

½ cup soy sauce

½ cup honey

1 garlic clove, minced

1½ teaspoons ground ginger

1 tablespoon cornstarch

In a large skillet, heat the oil over medium-high heat. Brown the beef, then add the reserved mandarin orange liquid, the soy sauce, honey, garlic, and ginger; mix well. Reduce the heat to medium, cover, and cook for 10 to 15 minutes, or until the beef is tender, stirring occasionally. Remove 2 tablespoons of the liquid from the skillet and combine with the cornstarch in a small bowl. Add the cornstarch mixture and the oranges to the skillet, stirring until the sauce thickens. Serve immediately.

GREAT GO-ALONG:
While the beef is cooking, make a batch of instant white rice to serve it over. And give it some crunch by topping it all with store-bought Chinese crispy noodles.

Country-French Patties

1½ pounds ground beef

½ cup Italian-flavored bread crumbs

1 medium onion, chopped

1 egg

½ teaspoon black pepper

1 can (10¾ ounces) condensed cream of mushroom soup

¾ cup milk

½ pound sliced fresh mushrooms

Everybody's fallen into a ground beef rut at one time or another. It seems that hamburgers and meat loaf are regular items on many families' menus. There are really so many other ways to prepare ground beef . . . and this recipe's just the beginning!

In a large bowl, combine the ground beef, bread crumbs, onion, egg, and pepper; mix well. Shape into six ½-inch-thick oval patties. Heat a large skillet over medium-high heat and place the patties in the skillet. Cook for 2 to 3 minutes per side, or until browned. In a small bowl, combine the mushroom soup, milk, and mushrooms; mix well and pour over the patties. Reduce the heat to medium-low, cover, and simmer for 8 to 10 minutes, or until the beef is no longer pink. Serve topped with the mushroom sauce.

FAMILY DINNER

97

GREAT GO-ALONG:
While the patties are simmering, whip up some instant mashed potatoes and stir in some grated Cheddar cheese, and dinner will be complete.

Cheeseburger Bake

Tired of flipping burgers? Here's how you can get that great cheeseburger taste without cooking separate burgers for everybody. And the cook gets to sit down and eat with the rest of the gang, too!

1½ pounds lean ground beef

1½ teaspoons onion powder

½ teaspoon garlic powder

½ teaspoon black pepper

⅓ cup ketchup

1½ cups (6 ounces) finely shredded sharp Cheddar cheese

1 package (7½ ounces) refrigerated biscuits (10 biscuits)

Preheat the oven to 450°F. Coat an 8-inch square baking dish with nonstick cooking spray. In a large skillet, brown the ground beef with the onion powder, garlic powder, and pepper over high heat, stirring to break up the beef. Drain off any fat, then add the ketchup and cheese; mix well and pour into the baking dish. Place the biscuits over the top and bake for 8 to 10 minutes, or until the biscuits are golden and cooked through.

> **GREAT GO-ALONG:**
> Heat a package of frozen steak fries in the oven at the same time this is baking. Give them a shot of nonstick cooking spray before baking for an extra-crispy crunch.

Beat-the-Clock Goulash

6 SERVINGS

On your mark, get set, cook! You're gonna be at the finish line . . . and ready before the family gets to the table!

2 pounds lean ground beef

1 medium onion, chopped

2 cans (14½ ounces each) ready-to-use beef broth

1 package (8 ounces) elbow macaroni

1 tablespoon paprika

1 tablespoon garlic powder

1 teaspoon black pepper

1 cup sour cream

In a soup pot, brown the ground beef with the onion over high heat, stirring to break up the beef. Add the broth, macaroni, paprika, garlic powder, and pepper and bring to a boil, stirring occasionally. Reduce the heat to medium-high, cover, and simmer for 6 to 8 minutes, or until the macaroni is tender. Remove from the heat; stir in the sour cream and serve in bowls.

TO FANCY IT UP:
Sprinkle with chopped fresh parsley and an extra shake or two of paprika just before serving.

TIMESAVING TIP:
Buy an extra set of metal measuring spoons, remove them from the ring, and store them on a magnetic strip by your spice rack. Then you simply have to wash the one you use instead of the whole set.

Ravioli Cacciatore

No need to worry about all the messy pots and pans ravioli usually leaves behind, because this version is a one-pan wonder, filled with lots of saucy, meaty, cheesy good taste.

1 jar (26 ounces) spaghetti sauce

½ cup water

2 medium onions, cut in half, then sliced

2 medium green bell peppers, cut into thin strips

1 package (25 ounces) frozen beef-filled ravioli, thawed

1 cup (4 ounces) shredded mozzarella cheese

In a soup pot or deep skillet, bring the spaghetti sauce, water, onions, and bell peppers to a boil over medium-high heat. Add the ravioli; mix well. Reduce the heat to medium-low, cover, and cook for 10 to 15 minutes, or until the ravioli are tender, stirring frequently. Sprinkle the cheese over the ravioli. Cover and cook for 1 minute, or until the cheese melts. Serve immediately.

FAMILY DINNER

100

GREAT GO-ALONG:
Add some cherry tomatoes and red onion to a prepared bagged salad mix, then top with a tangy Italian dressing to round out your meal-in-minutes.

Smothered Pork Chops

4 SERVINGS

½ cup all-purpose flour

¼ teaspoon garlic powder

4 pork loin chops (1½ to 2 pounds total)

2 tablespoons vegetable oil

1 can (10¾ ounces) condensed cream of mushroom soup

1 can (8 ounces) mushroom stems and pieces, drained

¾ cup milk

1 container (2.8 ounces) French-fried onions

What makes a smothered pork chop? Loads of creamy mushroom soup and mushrooms and . . . oh yes, a whole lotta good taste.

In a shallow dish, combine the flour and garlic powder; mix well. Coat the pork chops completely with the seasoned flour. Heat the oil in a large skillet and brown the pork chops over high heat for 2 to 3 minutes per side. Add the soup, mushrooms, and milk; mix well and bring to a boil. Reduce the heat to medium, cover, and cook for 15 to 18 minutes, or until the pork chops are cooked through and tender. Sprinkle with the onions and serve.

GREAT GO-ALONG:
Boil up some curly egg noodles and ladle on some of this creamy sauce.

Twenty-Minute Italian Chili

6 TO 8 SERVINGS

Chili is one of those dishes that's got lots of tasty variations. We can make vegetarian chili with beans and fresh veggies. We can even toss leftover hamburgers and hot dogs with tomatoes and beans for a quick leftover chili. And here's another one—Italian-style chili brimming with loads of our favorite tastes.

1 pound boneless, skinless chicken thighs, cut into ½-inch chunks

½ pound Italian sausage, casings removed

1 medium onion, chopped

3 cans (14½ ounces each) Italian stewed tomatoes, undrained

2 cans (15 ounces each) cannellini beans, undrained

2 tablespoons chili powder

1 teaspoon ground cumin

¼ teaspoon salt

In a soup pot, cook the chicken, sausage, and onion over high heat for 5 to 6 minutes, or until browned, stirring to break up the sausage. Stir in the remaining ingredients and bring to a boil. Reduce the heat to medium and cook for 15 minutes, stirring occasionally.

TO FANCY IT UP:
Top each bowl with a sprig of fresh basil and a sprinkle of grated Parmesan cheese.

Marmalade Dijon Pork Chops

4 SERVINGS

These jazzed-up pork chops are much better than regular pork chops—and tangier, too. This oughta make you a dinnertime hero.

1 jar (12 ounces) orange marmalade
¼ cup orange juice
3 tablespoons Dijon-style mustard
¼ cup all-purpose flour
¼ teaspoon salt
¼ teaspoon black pepper
4 pork loin chops (1½ to 2 pounds total)
2 tablespoons vegetable oil

In a medium bowl, combine the marmalade, orange juice, and mustard; mix well and set aside. In a shallow dish, combine the flour, salt, and pepper; mix well. Coat the pork chops with the seasoned flour. Heat the oil in a large deep skillet over medium-high heat. Add the pork chops and brown for 3 to 4 minutes per side. Reduce the heat to low, pour the marmalade sauce over the top, cover, and simmer for 5 minutes. Uncover and simmer for 5 to 7 more minutes, or until the sauce is thickened and the pork chops are no longer pink. Serve with the sauce spooned over the chops.

GREAT GO-ALONG:
Mix up that box of wild rice you've got in your pantry for a super-satisfying side dish.

Country Barbecue Ribs

"Slow-cooked" often goes along with ribs, but not this time. And during the short time these ribs are cooking, steam some corn on the cob and boil a few potatoes. Then in less than 30 minutes, you'll have your own slow-cooked-tasting barbecue!

3 TO 4 SERVINGS

2½ to 3 pounds boneless country-style pork ribs

½ cup ketchup

½ cup honey

¼ cup soy sauce

8 garlic cloves, minced

In a large skillet, cook the ribs over high heat for 4 to 5 minutes, turning to brown on all sides. In a small bowl, combine the remaining ingredients; mix well, then add to the skillet and bring to a boil. Reduce the heat to medium-high, cover, and cook for 18 to 20 minutes, or until the ribs are tender. Serve with the sauce spooned over the ribs.

TIMESAVING TIP: A tablespoon of bottled chopped garlic can easily replace the minced cloves.

Fancy Fast Greek Chicken

1 tablespoon vegetable oil

6 boneless, skinless chicken breast halves (1½ to 2 pounds total)

½ teaspoon salt

1 jar (12 ounces) chicken gravy

¼ cup dry white wine

1½ teaspoons fresh lemon juice

1 can (2¼ ounces) sliced black olives, drained

1½ teaspoons dried oregano

Turn ordinary chicken into a Mediterranean specialty simply by adding lemon juice, olives, and white wine. See how easy it is?

Heat the oil in a large skillet over medium-high heat. Season the chicken with the salt, then cook it for 3 to 4 minutes per side, or until browned. In a small bowl, combine the remaining ingredients; mix well. Pour over the chicken and simmer for 4 to 5 minutes, or until no pink remains in the chicken. Serve immediately.

FAMILY DINNER

105

TO FANCY IT UP:
Top with crumbled feta cheese and additional sliced black olives.

Polynesian Chicken

After a stressful day, don't you want something that'll transport you to a faraway place? How about a trip to the tropics? Dig into this dish and you're there!

1½ pounds boneless, skinless chicken breasts, cut into 1-inch chunks

½ teaspoon salt

⅛ teaspoon black pepper

2 tablespoons vegetable oil

1½ cups sweet-and-sour sauce

1 can (8 ounces) pineapple chunks, drained

2 bell peppers (1 each red and green), cut into 1-inch chunks

½ cup maraschino cherries, drained

Season the chicken with the salt and pepper. Heat the oil in a large skillet over high heat. Cook the chicken for 8 to 10 minutes, or until no pink remains, stirring occasionally. Reduce the heat to medium-low and add the remaining ingredients; mix well. Cook for 3 to 5 minutes, or until heated through. Serve immediately.

GREAT GO-ALONG:
A big pot of quick-cooking brown rice will team up perfectly with this. And what do you say to a piña colada to wash it all down?

Chicken Vegetable Penne

1 pound penne pasta

1 tablespoon vegetable oil

1½ pounds boneless, skinless chicken breasts, cut into 1-inch chunks

½ teaspoon salt

2 medium zucchini, cut into ½-inch chunks

1 jar (12 ounces) chicken gravy

1 pint cherry tomatoes, halved

½ cup grated Parmesan cheese

Many times I've referred to pasta as "fast food." There are really two reasons for that—one is because it's ready so fast and the other is because the gang eats it so fast! And we can be sure that this fast chicken-and-pasta favorite will get eaten up before we can call, "Dinnertime!"

Cook the pasta according to the package directions; drain and return to the pot. Meanwhile, heat the oil in a large skillet over medium-high heat. Season the chicken with the salt, then cook for 5 to 7 minutes, until browned. Add the zucchini and cook for 6 to 8 minutes, or until crisp-tender. Add the gravy; mix well and cook until heated through and no pink remains in the chicken. Add the chicken mixture, cherry tomatoes, and cheese to the pasta and toss until well combined. Serve immediately.

FAMILY DINNER

107

GREAT GO-ALONG:
What's an Italian meal without bread? So serve a loaf of Italian bread and, instead of the usual plain butter, make a seasoned olive oil for dipping. Just pour some olive oil onto a shallow plate, top it with grated Parmesan cheese, oregano, basil, and/or black pepper, and dip away!

Crispy Fish 'n' Chips

Nope, this isn't the traditional English-style fish and chips. This time we're gonna do things a little differently by rolling the fish in potato chips, then baking it till it's extra-crispy.

1 package (5½ ounces) salt-and-vinegar-flavored potato chips, crushed

1 tablespoon chopped fresh parsley

¼ teaspoon black pepper

1½ pounds fresh or frozen white-fleshed fish fillets, such as cod, haddock, or whiting, thawed if frozen

¼ cup (½ stick) butter, melted

Preheat the oven to 425°F. Coat a baking sheet with nonstick cooking spray. In a shallow dish, combine the crushed potato chips, parsley, and pepper; mix well. Brush both sides of the fish with the melted butter, then coat with the potato chip mixture. Place on the baking sheet and bake for 15 to 20 minutes, or until the fish flakes easily with a fork. Serve immediately.

SO MANY OPTIONS!
Can't find salt-and-vinegar potato chips?
Any flavor can be used, from regular to sour-cream-and-onion, or even tangy barbecue.

Gobble-It-Up Spaghetti

6 TO 8 SERVINGS

¼ cup olive oil
2 large onions, chopped
4 garlic cloves, minced
1 pound turkey sausage, casings removed
2 medium zucchini, chopped
1 jar (26 ounces) spaghetti sauce
2 large tomatoes, coarsely chopped
1 pound spaghetti

Only one thing is more fun than experimenting in the kitchen, and that's sampling the results. Go ahead—sample away!

Heat the oil in a soup pot over high heat. Add the onions and garlic and sauté for 3 to 5 minutes, or until tender. Add the sausage and zucchini and cook for 5 minutes, or until the sausage is browned, stirring to break up the sausage. Add the spaghetti sauce and tomatoes and bring to a boil. Reduce the heat to medium and simmer for 5 to 6 minutes, or until heated through. Meanwhile, cook the spaghetti according to the package directions; drain. Toss the spaghetti with the sauce and serve.

TO MAKE IT EVEN EASIER:
Do it all in one pot! Make your spaghetti first, then rinse and let drain in the colander while preparing the sauce. Return the spaghetti to the pot, stir, and heat until warmed through.

TIMESAVING TIP:
Keep a big rubber dishpan under the sink. Then, when the whole gang comes over for dinner, you're ready to clear the dishes restaurant-style— all in just one trip!

Parmesan Turkey Meat Loaves

These days our supermarkets are selling all kinds of ground meats. We can buy everything from ground chicken to ground pork, veal, and even venison. How 'bout picking up some ground turkey breast on your next shopping trip? This is the perfect way to prepare it. (Then maybe next time you'll be brave enough to move on to something more exotic!)

3 SERVINGS

¾ pound
ground turkey breast

1 small onion, finely chopped

1 cup (4 ounces) shredded mozzarella cheese, divided

⅓ cup plus 2 tablespoons spaghetti sauce, divided

1 egg

3 tablespoons grated Parmesan cheese

2 tablespoons Italian-flavored bread crumbs

1 teaspoon Italian seasoning

Preheat the oven to 425°F. Coat a 6-cup muffin tin with non-stick cooking spray. In a large bowl, combine the ground turkey, onion, ¾ cup mozzarella cheese, ⅓ cup spaghetti sauce, the egg, Parmesan cheese, bread crumbs, and Italian seasoning; mix well. Divide the mixture equally among the muffin cups. Brush the tops with the remaining 2 tablespoons spaghetti sauce and sprinkle with the remaining ¼ cup mozzarella cheese. Bake for 20 to 25 minutes, or until no pink remains in the meat. Serve immediately.

> **TO MAKE IT A COMPLETE MEAL:**
> Cook up some penne pasta and heat additional spaghetti sauce to top it off.

Skillet Chicken Noodle Parmigiana

3 TO 4 SERVINGS

I bet you're gonna love this new way to use your noodles. Yup! This time they're made in a skillet, so cleanup's a snap!

1 tablespoon vegetable oil

1 package (9 ounces) frozen cooked Southern-fried chicken fillets, thawed

1 jar (26 ounces) spaghetti sauce

1½ cups water

½ pound sliced fresh mushrooms

2 packages (3 ounces each) ramen noodles, broken up

1 cup (4 ounces) shredded mozzarella cheese

Heat the oil in a large skillet over medium-high heat. Add the chicken and cook for 2 to 3 minutes per side, until browned. Remove the chicken to a platter and cover to keep warm. Add the remaining ingredients except the cheese to the skillet (reserve the seasoning packets from the noodles for another use). Cook for 4 to 5 minutes, or until the noodles are tender. Reduce the heat to medium-low and place the chicken over the noodles. Top with the mozzarella cheese, cover, and cook for 4 to 5 minutes, or until the cheese is melted and the chicken is heated through. Serve the chicken over the noodles.

GREAT GO-ALONG:
Start with a classic Italian salad of sliced tomato and fresh mozzarella drizzled with Italian vinaigrette dressing and topped with chopped fresh basil.

Creamy Crab Casserole

Tell the family you're making crab for a weeknight dinner and they'll be asking what the special occasion is. Just tell 'em you're celebrating a new shortcut recipe.

1 can (10¾ ounces) condensed cream of mushroom soup

1 cup sour cream

1 pound fresh or frozen imitation crabmeat, thawed if frozen, coarsely chopped

1 package (10 ounces) frozen asparagus spears, thawed, drained, and chopped

¼ teaspoon black pepper

2 cups crushed cheese-flavored crackers

⅓ cup butter, melted

Preheat the oven to 400°F. Coat an 8-inch square baking dish with nonstick cooking spray. In a large bowl, combine the soup, sour cream, crabmeat, asparagus, and pepper; mix well. Pour into the baking dish. In a small bowl, combine the cracker crumbs and butter; mix well and sprinkle over the crabmeat mixture. Bake for 15 to 20 minutes, or until heated through. Serve immediately.

SO MANY OPTIONS!
Although I chose asparagus for this, broccoli, spinach, or even a frozen vegetable mix will work, too.

Fish Parmigiana

4 TO 6 SERVINGS

3 tablespoons olive oil

1 package (18.7 ounces) frozen breaded fish fillets

1 jar (26 ounces) spaghetti sauce

3 tablespoons prepared white horseradish

2 cups (8 ounces) shredded mozzarella cheese

Sure, we've all heard of chicken, veal, and eggplant parmigiana, but a seafood-style parmigiana? Why not? Anything goes—especially when it's easy to make and tastes this good.

Heat the oil in a large skillet over high heat. Add the fish and cook for 3 minutes per side, or until golden and crisp. In a medium bowl, combine the spaghetti sauce and horseradish; mix well. Reduce the heat to medium, pour the sauce mixture over the fish, and sprinkle with the cheese. Cover and cook for 5 to 7 minutes, or until heated through.

TO MAKE IT A COMPLETE MEAL:
Toast some garlic bread and toss a salad ...
and you'll still have extra time before ringing
the dinner bell!

Shrimp "Fried" Rice

Most people would probably rather order Chinese food to take out than make it at home. But I'm willing to bet I can get you to change your mind with this easy recipe, especially because it combines all our favorite Chinese restaurant tastes with just a few easy steps.

2 tablespoons vegetable oil

2 cups uncooked instant rice

1 can (14½ ounces) ready-to-use chicken broth

1 package (10 ounces) frozen cooked salad shrimp, thawed

1 package (10 ounces) frozen peas, thawed

4 scallions, thinly sliced

2 tablespoons soy sauce

¼ teaspoon black pepper

Heat the oil in a large skillet over high heat. Add the rice and sauté for 5 to 7 minutes, or until browned, stirring occasionally. Add the broth and bring to a boil over high heat. Turn off the heat, cover, and let sit for 5 to 7 minutes, or until the broth has been absorbed. Stir in the remaining ingredients and cook for 4 to 6 minutes over medium heat, or until heated through and the liquid is absorbed. Serve immediately.

FAMILY DINNER

GREAT GO-ALONG:
Start the meal with a quick egg drop soup that you make by heating canned chicken broth with a touch of soy sauce. Slowly stir in a beaten egg until egg strands form. Top with sliced scallions and serve.

Stovetop Tuna Casserole

6 TO 8 SERVINGS

1 pound rigatoni pasta

2 cans (10¾ ounces each) condensed Cheddar cheese soup

2 cans (12 ounces each) tuna, drained and flaked

1 cup milk

½ teaspoon black pepper

1 package (6 ounces) potato chips, crushed

Think you've got nothing to make for dinner? Take a look inside your cupboards. I'm willing to bet you've got some pasta, tuna fish, and potato chips. Add some Cheddar cheese soup and, before you know it, you've got dinner!

In a soup pot, cook the pasta according to the package directions; drain and return to the pot. Add the soup, tuna, milk, and pepper; mix well. Cook over medium-high heat for 2 to 3 minutes, or until heated through. Sprinkle the crushed potato chips over the top and serve.

TO FANCY IT UP:
Serve it as a casserole. Just spoon the hot tuna mixture into a casserole dish, then top with the crushed potato chips. Grab a trivet and it's table-ready.

Clams Scampi

We can't go wrong with pasta. It makes a super-quick meal and it always tastes good. But tonight, let's do things a little bit differently. Instead of heating up plain spaghetti sauce, we're gonna sauté clams with garlic and lemon juice for a scampi that's out of this world and ready in no time.

1 pound linguine

½ cup (1 stick) butter

5 garlic cloves, minced

½ teaspoon salt

½ teaspoon black pepper

2 cans (10 ounces each) whole baby clams, drained

Juice of ½ lemon

1 tablespoon chopped fresh parsley

Cook the linguine according to the package directions; drain. Meanwhile, melt the butter in a large skillet over medium-low heat. Stir in the garlic, salt, and pepper and sauté for 2 to 3 minutes, or until the garlic is tender. Stir in the clams, lemon juice, and parsley; cook for 3 to 5 minutes, or until heated through. Pour over the linguine and serve.

TO MAKE IT A COMPLETE MEAL:
While you're mincing the garlic, mince a few extra cloves and combine it with softened salted butter. Spread that over a loaf of French bread that's been cut in half lengthwise. Wrap it in foil and bake at 350°F. while preparing the scampi.

Spinach Pasta Soufflé

4 TO 6 SERVINGS

1 pound bow-tie pasta

1 jar (17 ounces) Alfredo sauce

2 packages (12 ounces each) frozen spinach soufflé, thawed

Homemade baked pasta dishes always took lots of work. And even if the prep time wasn't long, they still had to bake for at least an hour or so. Okay, this is a spinach soufflé version that's a bit different from the usual baked pasta dishes, but it's a yummy and fast alternative.

Cook the pasta according to the package directions; drain and return to the pot. Add the Alfredo sauce and spinach soufflé; mix well. Cook over medium-high heat for 6 to 8 minutes, or until heated through, stirring frequently. Serve immediately.

One-Pot Macaroni and Cheese

Yup, it's a lightning-quick stovetop version of "mac and cheese," made with spaghetti. No spaghetti? Use ziti. No ziti? How about shells? See, that's the best part of this recipe—we can change it every time or keep it the same. But one thing doesn't change—the creamy, cheesy flavor.

4 TO 6 SERVINGS

1 pound spaghetti

¼ cup (½ stick) butter

½ cup all-purpose flour

4 cups (1 quart) milk

6 cups (24 ounces) shredded sharp Cheddar cheese

½ teaspoon dry mustard

1 teaspoon salt

1 teaspoon black pepper

In a soup pot, cook the spaghetti according to the package directions; drain and set aside in the colander. In the same pot, melt the butter over medium heat, then stir in the flour. Gradually stir in the milk and cook for 3 to 5 minutes, or until thickened, stirring frequently. Add the cheese, dry mustard, salt, and pepper and stir for 3 to 5 minutes, or until the cheese is melted. Add the spaghetti and cook for 2 to 3 minutes, or until heated through, stirring constantly. Serve immediately.

TIMESAVING TIP:
Put on a pot of water to boil when you walk through the door—even before reading the mail or changing your clothes. Then you're halfway to cooking your pasta, rice, or potatoes for dinner.

Vegetable Couscous

4 TO 6 SERVINGS

1 tablespoon olive oil

1 medium onion, chopped

1 can (14½ ounces) ready-to-use chicken broth

1 package (16 ounces) frozen mixed vegetables, thawed

1 medium tomato, chopped

1 tablespoon chopped fresh dill

1½ teaspoons garlic salt

1 package (10 ounces) couscous

Don't be intimidated by the name. Couscous is just another member of the grain family. And when it's mixed with colorful mixed veggies and fresh tomato, it's a family member we'll invite for dinner again and again.

Heat the olive oil in a soup pot over medium-high heat. Add the onion and cook for 5 to 6 minutes, or until golden. Stir in the chicken broth, mixed vegetables, tomato, dill, and garlic salt; bring to a boil. Boil for 2 minutes, stirring occasionally, then stir in the couscous. Cover and remove from the heat; let stand for 5 minutes. Fluff with a fork and serve.

HELPFUL HINT:
For a complete vegetarian meal, use vegetable broth in place of the chicken broth, and maybe add more fresh dill.

Dinner for Two

I'm the first one to admit that a night spent with the entire family can be a great time. But every once in a while we all need a little quiet time with our special someone. And I don't mean time spent doing housework or running errands . . . I mean quality time.

I've always said that quality time is best spent sharing a good meal. And to do that we shouldn't have to spend hours cooking and cleaning up. So how do we do it?

Easy! I've figured out how to scale down and prepare the absolute easiest versions of some of our favorite fancy dishes . . . just for two. Instead of last-minute chopping, mixing, and cooking, we can enjoy a glass of wine or sparkling juice, share uninterrupted conversation, and, best of all, dine on great-tasting, fancy-looking dishes that show that special someone just how much we care.

Dinner for Two

Porterhouse for Two   123

Mustard Steak Salad   124

Veal alla Patty   125

Herb-Crusted Rack of Lamb   126

Pork Tenderloin Marsala   127

Quick Chicken Francaise   128

Chicken Caesar Salad   129

Fruity Cornish Hens   130

Skillet Clambake   131

Potato-Crusted Salmon   132

Almost Lobster Tail   133

Sizzlin' Shrimp Stir-fry   134

Off-the-Skewer Chicken Kebabs   135

Spinach Fettuccine Primavera   136

Tortellini with Portobello Mushrooms   137

Porterhouse for Two

Here's the perfect excuse to serve an intimate dinner for you and your sweetheart—a main dish that's custom-made for two, just like the name says!

One 2-inch-thick beef porterhouse steak (about 2 pounds)

3 tablespoons vegetable oil, divided

1 teaspoon salt

½ teaspoon black pepper

2 medium onions, thinly sliced

3 garlic cloves, minced

Rub the steak with 1 tablespoon vegetable oil, the salt, and pepper. Heat the remaining 2 tablespoons oil in a large skillet over high heat. Add the steak and place the onions and garlic around it. Brown the steak for about 3 minutes. Reduce the heat to medium, then turn the steak and onions over; cover and cook for 10 to 12 minutes for medium-rare, or until steak reaches desired doneness and onions are golden. Cut the beef away from the bone, slice across the grain, and serve topped with the caramelized onions.

DINNER FOR TWO

123

GREAT GO-ALONG:
What's a better side dish than creamed spinach—and it's so easy! Just sauté a chopped onion in a little butter and add a package of frozen spinach that's been thawed and drained, salt (if desired), pepper, and ½ cup heavy cream. Stir until hot and thickened.

Mustard Steak Salad

It's another hot summer night, the kids are all at sleepovers, and we're looking for a refreshing dinner to enjoy on the back porch. This salad may be light, but when you add the steak, it's a perfect summer meal.

One ¾-pound flank steak

2 tablespoons Dijon-style mustard

1 garlic clove, minced

¼ teaspoon black pepper

¾ cup Italian dressing

1 package (16 ounces) mixed salad greens

2 plum tomatoes, cut into wedges

Coat a medium skillet with nonstick cooking spray. Using a knife, score the steak diagonally on both sides, making a crisscross pattern. In a small bowl, combine the mustard, garlic, and pepper; mix well and rub over both sides of the steak. Heat the skillet over high heat. Add the steak and cook for 4 to 5 minutes per side for medium-rare, or until desired doneness. Remove the steak to a cutting board and thinly slice across the grain. Add the Italian dressing to the skillet and stir to combine with the pan drippings. Divide the salad and tomatoes between two plates. Top with the sliced steak and drizzle with the warm dressing mixture. Serve immediately.

HELPFUL HINT:
To cut the tartness of the dressing, mix a tablespoon or two of sugar into it as it's heating.

Veal alla Patty

¼ cup all-purpose flour

1 egg, beaten

2 tablespoons butter

½ pound veal cutlets, pounded to a ¼-inch thickness

1 can (14 ounces) artichokes, drained and chopped

½ cup sun-dried tomatoes in oil, drained and chopped

⅓ cup dry vermouth or white wine

Juice of ½ lemon

I had to name this scrumptious dish after our test kitchen veteran Patty. This dish was her idea, and if anybody knows how to put a quick meal together, plus make it extra-special, Patty sure does. Don't pass up this one.

Place the flour and egg in separate shallow dishes. Melt the butter in a large skillet over medium heat. Coat the veal in the flour, then in the egg, coating completely. Cook the veal for 2 to 3 minutes per side, or until golden. Stir in the artichokes, sun-dried tomatoes, vermouth, and lemon juice. Cook for 2 to 3 minutes, or until the sauce is thickened. Serve immediately.

GREAT GO-ALONG:
Patty suggests starting this meal with a salad of mixed baby greens (you can buy it ready-made), topped with slices of plum tomatoes and fresh mozzarella cheese. Ooh-la-la!

Herb-Crusted Rack of Lamb

2 SERVINGS

Rack of lamb is one of those dishes we think we could never make at home and that, even if we could, would take hours. My answer to that? Never say never! Once you see how easy this is, you're gonna be making it regularly.

½ teaspoon dried rosemary

½ teaspoon dried thyme

½ teaspoon salt

¼ teaspoon black pepper

One 1½- to 2-pound rack of lamb, cut in half

½ cup herb-seasoned crumb stuffing

2 tablespoons butter, melted

Preheat the oven to 450°F. In a small bowl, combine the rosemary, thyme, salt, and pepper; mix well and use to season all sides of the lamb, coating completely. Place in a roasting pan, top with the crumb stuffing, and drizzle with the butter. Bake for 20 to 25 minutes for medium-rare, or until desired doneness. Cut into individual chops and serve.

DINNER FOR TWO

126

> ### GREAT GO-ALONG:
> While the rack of lamb is baking, steam some broccoli florets and make a shortcut béarnaise sauce for them by combining ½ cup mayonnaise, 1 tablespoon white vinegar, 1 teaspoon dried tarragon, ¼ teaspoon dried parsley, and ⅛ teaspoon garlic powder.

Pork Tenderloin Marsala

2 SERVINGS

They say it's more fun to share, so wait until you share this juicy tenderloin with your favorite someone. You'll both agree—this one's a winner.

2 tablespoons all-purpose flour
½ teaspoon salt
⅛ teaspoon black pepper
One 14- to 16-ounce pork tenderloin
3 tablespoons olive oil
½ pound sliced fresh mushrooms
2 medium onions, thinly sliced
½ cup sweet Marsala wine

In a shallow dish, combine the flour, salt, and pepper; mix well. Coat the pork tenderloin with the mixture. Heat the oil in a soup pot over medium-high heat. Add the tenderloin and cook for 6 to 8 minutes, turning to brown all sides; remove to a platter and set aside. Add the mushrooms and onions to the pot and sauté for 6 to 8 minutes, or until tender, stirring occasionally; stir in the wine. Return the tenderloin to the pot and cook for 6 to 8 minutes, or until cooked through. Slice the tenderloin and serve topped with the mushrooms and onions.

DINNER FOR TWO

127

GREAT GO-ALONG:
Make a flavored rice dish from one of the packages you've got buried in your pantry.

Quick Chicken Francaise

Oh boy! You'll feel like a fancy French chef when you serve this classic dish. And even though we're saving time, we certainly aren't skimping on taste. As the French always say, "Bon appétit!"

2 SERVINGS

2 tablespoons butter

½ pound sliced fresh mushrooms

1 package (9 ounces) frozen fully cooked breaded chicken breast fillets, thawed

⅔ cup dry white wine

Juice of 1 lemon

1 tablespoon all-purpose flour

¼ teaspoon black pepper

Melt the butter in a large skillet over medium-high heat. Add the mushrooms and sauté for 2 to 3 minutes. Add the chicken fillets and cook for 3 to 4 minutes per side, or until crisp. In a small bowl, combine the remaining ingredients; mix well. Stir into the skillet and cook for 2 to 3 minutes, or until heated through and the sauce has thickened. Serve immediately.

GREAT GO-ALONG:
Boil up some angel hair pasta, then drain it and give it a quick toss with some butter, chopped parsley, and garlic powder.

Chicken Caesar Salad

2 SERVINGS

¼ cup
Italian-flavored bread crumbs

1 package (1.2 ounces) dry Caesar
dressing mix, divided

1 egg, beaten

2 boneless, skinless chicken breast halves
(½ to ¾ pound total), pounded
to a ¼-inch thickness

¼ cup plus 2 tablespoons olive oil, divided

3 tablespoons white vinegar

½ head romaine lettuce,
cut into bite-sized pieces

1 tablespoon *shredded*
Parmesan cheese

*Surprise! This is it—the
perfect summertime meal.
Light a few candles, serve
dinner on the patio, and
add a bottle of white wine.*

In a shallow dish, combine the bread crumbs and 2 tablespoons of the Caesar dressing mix; mix well. Place the egg in another shallow dish. Dip the chicken in the egg, then in the bread crumb mixture, coating completely. Heat 2 tablespoons of the oil in a large skillet over medium-high heat. Add the chicken and cook for 3 to 4 minutes per side, or until golden. Meanwhile, in a small bowl, whisk the vinegar and the remaining Caesar dressing mix and ¼ cup oil; mix well. Toss with the romaine lettuce, then place on a platter, top with the chicken, and sprinkle with the Parmesan cheese. Serve immediately.

> **TO KEEP THINGS EXCITING:**
> Start off with an appetizer of cantaloupe wedges wrapped in prosciutto or other Italian ham. It's a classic . . . one that's very refreshing.

Fruity Cornish Hens

Forget serving ordinary baked chicken tonight. We want something new and exciting for dinner. So how 'bout bringing some colorful fruit flavor to the table? And when it's a fruity glaze over fancy Cornish game hens, it's a five-star meal . . . fast, fast, fast.

2 Cornish hens, each cut in half

2 tablespoons sugar

½ teaspoon ground red pepper

2 tablespoons vegetable oil

1 can (15¼ ounces) fruit cocktail in heavy syrup, drained, with syrup reserved

1 can (10½ ounces) condensed chicken broth

¼ cup orange marmalade

1 tablespoon cornstarch

Season the Cornish hens with the sugar and ground red pepper. Heat the oil in a large skillet over high heat. Add the Cornish hens breast side down and brown for 4 to 5 minutes. Turn the hens over and add the reserved fruit cocktail syrup and the chicken broth. Cover and cook for 18 minutes. Uncover and add the fruit cocktail, marmalade, and cornstarch; mix well. Cook for 1 to 2 minutes, or until the sauce is thickened and no pink remains in the hens.

GREAT GO-ALONG:
This meal wouldn't be complete without a steaming bowl of wild rice . . . and it's nice sprinkled with slivered almonds.

HELPFUL HINT:
To make this even easier, ask the butcher to cut the Cornish hens for you . . . even if they're frozen.

Skillet Clambake

2 SERVINGS

3 cups water
6 small new potatoes
1 teaspoon salt
4 ears fresh corn, husked
2 dozen littleneck clams, cleaned
¼ cup (½ stick) butter, melted

Want to make a clambake for two without a big production? Make it skillet-style. It's fast, easy, and tasty . . . just how it should be.

In a large deep skillet, combine the water, potatoes, and salt over high heat. Cover and cook for 18 to 20 minutes, or until the potatoes are almost fork-tender. Add the corn and clams. Cover and cook for 5 minutes, or until the clams open. **Discard any clams that do not open.** Serve with the melted butter for dipping.

> **GREAT GO-ALONG:**
> For dessert, how about making s'mores by stacking graham crackers with pieces of a chocolate bar and marshmallows? Just microwave them for a few seconds, until the chocolate and marshmallows are all gooey. Be ready to eat 'em right away!

Potato-Crusted Salmon

Dim the lights, turn on the soft music, and prepare to enjoy this yummy dish. Yup, it's salmon crusted with potatoes. And wait till you see how 1–2–3 easy it is!

⅓ cup instant mashed potato flakes

¼ teaspoon onion powder

¼ teaspoon salt

¼ teaspoon black pepper

Two 6-ounce salmon fillets

¼ cup (½ stick) butter, melted

Preheat the oven to 350°F. Coat a 7" × 11" baking dish with non-stick cooking spray. In a shallow dish, combine the potato flakes, onion powder, salt, and pepper; mix well. Dip the fillets in the melted butter, then coat with the potato mixture and place in the baking dish. Sprinkle any remaining potato mixture evenly over the top. Drizzle the remaining butter over the fillets. Bake for 20 to 25 minutes, or until the fish flakes easily with a fork and the potato crust is golden. Serve immediately.

> **GREAT GO-ALONG:**
> While the salmon is baking, steam about ½ pound fresh asparagus. Let it cool slightly, then top it with a vinaigrette dressing made by combining balsamic vinegar, olive oil, salt, and pepper in an empty bottle and giving it all a shake.

Almost Lobster Tail

2 SERVINGS

2 tablespoons butter, melted
¼ teaspoon paprika
⅛ teaspoon salt
⅛ teaspoon black pepper
Two 6-ounce monkfish fillets
1 tablespoon plain bread crumbs

Who can resist the rich taste of lobster? Unfortunately, it's a bit on the pricey side—so I've got just the solution! Some call it "poor man's lobster," but I call it another way to say, "OOH IT'S SO GOOD!!®"

Preheat the oven to 350°F. In a small bowl, combine the butter, paprika, salt, and pepper; mix well. Place the fish on a baking sheet and brush evenly with the butter mixture. Sprinkle the bread crumbs evenly down the center of the fish fillets and bake for 15 to 17 minutes, or until the fish flakes easily with a fork. Serve immediately.

HELPFUL HINT:
Monkfish can be found in most fish stores and supermarket fish departments. If you don't see it, ask for it.

GREAT GO-ALONG:
A big baked potato will round out the meal and, oh—don't forget the melted butter for dipping the fish!

Sizzlin' Shrimp Stir-fry

Pick up some shrimp, then make a quick stop at the produce counter for all the fixin's for this Chinese favorite.

2 SERVINGS

2 tablespoons vegetable oil

1 garlic clove, minced

½ medium red bell pepper, cut into thin strips

¼ pound snow peas, trimmed

¼ pound sliced fresh mushrooms

1 pound large shrimp, peeled and deveined

1 tablespoon soy sauce

¼ teaspoon black pepper

Heat the oil in a large wok or skillet over high heat. Add the garlic and sauté until tender. Add the red pepper, snow peas, and mushrooms and stir-fry for 2 minutes. Add the remaining ingredients and stir-fry for 2 to 3 minutes, or until the shrimp are pink and the vegetables are crisp-tender. Serve immediately.

FOR A CHANGE OF PACE:
Use hoisin sauce in place of the soy. It makes a richer glaze.

GREAT GO-ALONG:
Pick up an order of steamed white rice from the nearby Chinese restaurant on the way home. It's reasonably priced and great-tasting!

Off-the-Skewer Chicken Kebabs

2 SERVINGS

1 large onion,
cut into wedges

1 large red bell pepper,
cut into 1-inch chunks

¾ pound boneless, skinless
chicken breasts, cut into 1-inch chunks

½ teaspoon garlic powder

¼ teaspoon ground ginger

½ teaspoon salt

1 can (8 ounces) pineapple chunks,
drained

¼ cup pineapple preserves

Kebabs are fun to eat, but sometimes it just doesn't make sense to spend time putting the veggies and chicken on a kebab only to take them off once they're cooked. Here's an un-shish-kebab kebab. It might sound strange, but try it.

Coat a large skillet with nonstick cooking spray and heat over high heat. Add the onion and red pepper. Cook for 3 to 4 minutes, or until browned, stirring occasionally. Season the chicken with the garlic powder, ginger, and salt. Add to the skillet and cook for 3 to 4 minutes, or until the chicken is browned, stirring occasionally. Add the pineapple chunks and preserves; mix well. Cook for 2 to 3 minutes, or until heated through and the chicken is no longer pink inside. Serve immediately.

DINNER FOR TWO

135

TO KEEP THINGS EXCITING:
Get out the blender and make a jumbo piña colada for two. Don't forget the straws!

Spinach Fettuccine Primavera

2 SERVINGS

Mamma mia, fettuccine primavera sounds pretty complicated. Guess what? It's really pretty easy. One bite of that rich and creamy fettuccine and you'll be singing your own Italian love song.

½ pound spinach fettuccine

3 tablespoons butter

1 package (16 ounces) frozen cauliflower, broccoli, and carrot mix, thawed and drained

2 tablespoons all-purpose flour

½ teaspoon salt

¼ teaspoon black pepper

1½ cups heavy cream

1 cup (4 ounces) shredded Italian cheese blend

Cook the fettuccine according to the package directions; drain. Meanwhile, melt the butter in a large skillet over medium heat. Add the vegetable mix and sauté for 2 minutes. Sprinkle the flour, salt, and pepper over the vegetables and sauté for 2 minutes. Add the heavy cream and cheese, stirring until the cheese melts. Toss the fettuccine with the cream sauce and serve.

> **TO KEEP THINGS EXCITING:**
> While the fettuccine is cooking, cut a loaf of French bread into diagonal slices, slather with garlic butter, and sprinkle with shredded Italian cheese blend or Parmesan cheese. Place on a baking sheet and bake at 375°F. until golden and the cheese is melted.

Tortellini with Portobello Mushrooms

2 SERVINGS

1 package (9 ounces) fresh cheese-filled tortellini

6 tablespoons (¾ stick) butter, divided

4 garlic cloves, minced

3 portobello mushroom caps (about 6 ounces), sliced

⅓ cup shredded Parmesan cheese

2 tablespoons chopped fresh basil, divided

⅛ teaspoon salt

¼ teaspoon black pepper

In the past, portobello mushrooms were found only at fancy gourmet stores. Lucky for us, these days they can be found right next to the white mushrooms at our super-market produce counters. And when they're served up hearty like this . . . boy, are we in for a treat!

Cook the tortellini according to the package directions; drain and return to the pot. Meanwhile, melt 3 tablespoons butter in a large skillet over medium heat. Add the garlic and sauté for 2 minutes. Add the mushrooms and sauté for 4 to 6 minutes, or until tender, stirring frequently. Add the remaining 3 tablespoons butter, the Parmesan cheese, 1 tablespoon basil, the salt, and pepper to the skillet; mix well. Serve the tortellini topped with the sautéed mushrooms and sprinkled with the remaining 1 tablespoon basil.

TIMESAVING TIP: Let kitchen scissors save you work and time—simply snip fresh herbs instead of chopping them.

Dessert

Moist chocolate cake. Homemade apple pie with fresh whipped cream. Ice cream sundaes with just the right mix of toppings. Yup, I bet most of us would agree that dessert is a pretty important part of any meal. It's that sweet ending we crave once the table is cleared and the dishes are stacked in the sink. And with all that we have cooking already, who has the time to make homemade desserts?

To some, cooking from scratch means defrosting a pie, baking a cake from a mix, or even taking the lid off a bakery item. That's okay

most of the time. But every so often we crave old-fashioned homemade taste, 'cause there's nothing like our own sweet treats, prepared right in our kitchens.

So say good-bye to long hours of mixing, rolling, and baking, 'cause I've created a whole new batch of grand dessert finales! Trust me, they're easy as can be and great-tasting, too. C'mon—roll up your sleeves and get to it. You're about to enjoy some of the best-tasting desserts around . . . yup, all made in just minutes.

Dessert

Strawberry Patch Shortcake   143

Pink Lemonade Pie   144

Chocolate Caramel Swirl Pie   145

Chocolate Raspberry Soufflé   146

Upside-Down Strawberry Cheesecake   147

Lemon Cream Tarts   148

Tropical Angel Food Cake   149

White Chocolate Macadamia Mousse   150

Raspberry-Almond-Mocha Torte   151

Black Forest Ice Cream Cake   152

Just-Your-Size Baked Alaska   153

Banana Rockets   154

Brandied Peach Parfait   155

Instant Strawberry Sorbet   156

Chilled Peaches 'n' Cream Soup   157

Fruit Stand Surprise   158

Tortilla Crepes   159

Lightning-Quick Baklava   160

Sweet Endings Pizza   161

Orange Cocoa Sandies   162

Cocoa Peanut Drops   163

Mocha Almond Truffles   164

Rocky Road Popcorn Balls   165

Strawberry Patch Shortcake

8 SERVINGS

1 package
(17.3 ounces) refrigerated
biscuits (8 biscuits)

1 tablespoon butter, melted

3 tablespoons sugar, divided

¼ teaspoon ground cinnamon

1 cup (½ pint) heavy cream

1 quart fresh strawberries, washed,
hulled, and halved

½ cup strawberry preserves, melted

This shortcut recipe makes short work of shortcake. Why, your gang will think you spent hours baking, but we'll keep that a secret.

Place the biscuits on a baking sheet and brush the tops with the melted butter. In a small bowl, combine 1 tablespoon sugar and the cinnamon; mix well and sprinkle over the tops of the biscuits. Bake according to the package directions and let cool. Meanwhile, in a medium bowl, beat the heavy cream and remaining 2 tablespoons sugar until stiff peaks form. Split the biscuits. Place the strawberries equally over the biscuit bottoms, reserving a few for garnish. Top with half of the whipped cream, replace the biscuit tops, and then top with the remaining whipped cream and the reserved strawberries. Drizzle with the strawberry preserves and serve.

FOR A CHANGE OF PACE: Replace the strawberries with blueberries and the strawberry preserves with blueberry. (I know this version will disappear in no time, too, since there are a bunch of blueberry lovers in my family.)

DESSERT

143

Pink Lemonade Pie

Here's one that'll make you feel like a kid with a lemonade stand . . . only this time you'll need a fork instead of a straw. And the best part? Cutting into this yummy pie won't mean cutting into the profits!

6 TO 8 SERVINGS

1 package (8 ounces) cream cheese, softened

1 container (6 ounces) frozen pink lemonade concentrate, thawed

1 container (8 ounces) frozen whipped topping, thawed

4 drops red food color (optional)

One 9-inch prepared shortbread pie crust

In a medium bowl, beat the cream cheese until smooth. Add the lemonade concentrate and beat until well combined. Stir in the whipped topping and food color, if desired. Spoon into the pie crust and freeze for 20 minutes. Serve, or cover and chill until ready to serve.

TO FANCY IT UP:
Just before serving, garnish with dollops of whipped cream and lemon slices.

HELPFUL HINT:
Oops, you left the pie in the freezer for longer than 20 minutes! That's okay; it tastes great frozen, too.

Chocolate Caramel Swirl Pie

1 package (8 ounces)
cream cheese, softened

1 package (4-serving size) chocolate
instant pudding and pie filling

½ cup milk

1 container (8 ounces) frozen
whipped topping, thawed, divided

One 9-inch chocolate graham
cracker pie crust

4 tablespoons caramel-flavored
topping, divided

Making a fancy dessert used to mean lots of time in the kitchen, plus lots of time shopping for all the ingredients we'd need. No more! With this pie, we'll save time in the kitchen and *be able to use the express checkout at the supermarket.*

In a large bowl, beat the cream cheese for 2 to 3 minutes, or until creamy. Slowly add the pudding mix and milk and continue beating until smooth. Add 2 cups whipped topping and stir until well blended. Spoon into the pie crust. Drizzle with 3 tablespoons caramel topping and use a knife to swirl it into the cream cheese mixture. Completely cover the top of the pie with the remaining whipped topping. Drizzle with the remaining 1 tablespoon caramel topping and freeze for 15 minutes. Serve, or cover and refrigerate until ready to serve.

> **FOR A CHANGE OF PACE:**
> Turn this into a turtle pie by stirring some chopped walnuts or pecans into the pudding mixture.

DESSERT

Chocolate Raspberry Soufflé

At five o'clock we can't expect everybody to tiptoe around the kitchen simply because there's a soufflé in the oven. With this one, they won't have to. As a matter of fact, the only tiptoeing anybody will be doing is into the kitchen . . . for seconds!

12 SERVINGS

3 eggs, separated

1 package (10 ounces) raspberry-flavored semisweet chocolate chips

½ cup (1 stick) butter

¼ cup plus 1 teaspoon sugar, divided

¼ cup water

½ cup heavy cream

½ teaspoon vanilla extract

Preheat the oven to 425°F. Line a 12-cup muffin tin with paper baking cups. In a medium bowl, beat the egg whites until stiff peaks form; set aside. In a medium saucepan, combine the chocolate chips, butter, ¼ cup sugar, and the water over medium heat. Cook for 2 to 3 minutes, or until the chocolate and butter have melted, stirring constantly. Remove from the heat and quickly whisk in the egg yolks. Add the beaten egg whites; fold until well combined. Pour evenly into the baking cups and bake for 8 to 10 minutes, or until puffed and the tops are dry. Meanwhile, in a medium bowl, beat the heavy cream with the remaining 1 teaspoon sugar and the vanilla until slightly thickened. Serve the warm soufflé with the vanilla cream sauce.

TO FANCY IT UP:
Just before serving, garnish each soufflé with fresh raspberries and a sprig of mint. Want to make these in advance? That works—just cover and chill; they taste just as good cold.

Upside-Down Strawberry Cheesecake

1 cup (½ pint) heavy cream

1 package (8 ounces) cream cheese, softened

1 package (4-serving size) vanilla instant pudding and pie filling mix

½ cup milk

2 tablespoons sugar

½ teaspoon lemon juice

1 pint fresh strawberries, washed, hulled, and halved

One 9-inch graham cracker pie crust, crumbled

Right side up or upside down, this is one creamy cheesecake that's a thumbs-up favorite time and time again.

In a medium bowl, beat the heavy cream until stiff peaks form; set aside. In a large bowl, beat the cream cheese until creamy. Add the pudding mix, milk, sugar, and lemon juice and continue beating until smooth. Add the whipped cream and stir until well blended. Place the strawberry halves in a 9-inch pie plate. Spoon the cream cheese mixture over them and top with the crumbled graham cracker crust. Serve, or cover and chill until ready to serve.

HELPFUL HINT:
For a conventional quick-and-easy strawberry cheesecake, just spoon the cream cheese filling into the pie crust and top with the strawberries.

DESSERT

147

Lemon Cream Tarts

*Uh-oh, the table is cleared
and the gang is asking about
dessert—and you forgot it!
Don't panic! In 5 minutes,
these tarts are table-ready.
Won't they be impressed!*

In a medium bowl,
combine all the ingre-
dients except the tart
shells; mix well. Spoon
into the tart shells and
serve, or keep chilled until
ready to serve.

6 SERVINGS

1 jar (10 ounces) lemon curd

1 container (8 ounces) frozen
whipped topping, thawed

1 teaspoon grated lemon peel
(optional)

5 drops yellow food color
(optional)

6 single-serve graham cracker
tart shells

HELPFUL HINT:

All it takes is passing a lemon over a grater
a few times and . . . ta da—you've got grated
lemon peel for using in the tarts as well as
for garnishing the tops.

Tropical Angel Food Cake

12 TO 16 SERVINGS

½ cup
sweetened flaked
coconut

1 can (8 ounces) pineapple tidbits,
drained

1 can (5 ounces) evaporated milk

½ cup (1 stick) butter

½ cup sugar

½ cup coarsely chopped macadamia nuts

One 10-inch prepared angel food cake

12 to 16 stemmed maraschino
cherries

One bite of this tropical delight instantly transports us to a far-off tropical island . . . and we can get there in just 20 minutes! Can you think of a more yummy escape?

In a medium skillet, toast the coconut over medium heat until golden, stirring constantly. Remove from the skillet and set aside. Add the pineapple, evaporated milk, butter, and sugar to the skillet; mix well and bring to a boil. Let boil for 5 to 7 minutes, or until thickened, stirring frequently. Return the coconut to the skillet and stir in the nuts. Remove from the heat. Slice the cake horizontally in half and spoon half of the pineapple mixture over the bottom half. Replace the cake top and top with the remaining pineapple mixture. Garnish with the cherries. Slice and serve, or cover and keep chilled until ready to serve.

FOR A CHANGE OF PACE:
Just add a scoop of low-fat frozen vanilla yogurt to serve this cake à la mode.

DESSERT

149

White Chocolate Macadamia Mousse

Can you imagine coming home, sorting through the mail, doing a load of laundry, and making dinner—including a fancy dessert—in 30 minutes? It can be done, and here's your grand finale!

6 TO 8 SERVINGS

1 package (6 ounces) white baking bars

2 tablespoons milk

1 cup coarsely chopped macadamia nuts

1 container (12 ounces) frozen whipped topping, thawed

In a medium saucepan, combine the baking bars and milk over low heat until the bars melt and the mixture is smooth, stirring constantly. Place in a medium bowl and stir in the nuts; mix well and allow to cool for 5 minutes. Gradually add the whipped topping, stirring until well blended. Serve, or cover and chill until ready to serve.

TO FANCY IT UP:
Spoon into stemmed wineglasses and crown with dollops of whipped topping and chocolate curls made by peeling a chocolate bar with a vegetable peeler. Yes, it's that easy.

Raspberry-Almond-Mocha Torte

10 TO 12 SERVINGS

One 16-ounce pound cake
½ cup raspberry preserves
1 tablespoon instant coffee granules
1 container (16 ounces) chocolate frosting
¼ cup sliced almonds

A torte is a pretty fancy-sounding dessert, huh? And for most people it means spending hours in the kitchen, mixing, baking, and layering. Say no more, because with just a few easy steps we've got our own torte that rivals any from a bakery. Your family will think you've found a new career as a pastry chef.

With a serrated knife, slice the pound cake into 5 horizontal slices. Place the bottom slice on a platter and spread a quarter of the preserves over the slice. Repeat three more times, then top with the final layer of pound cake. Stir the coffee granules into the container of frosting, mixing well. Spread over the top and sides of the cake, then sprinkle the top with the almonds.

SO MANY OPTIONS!
It's okay to use any flavor preserves. I even like to mix and match 'em—it's a great way to finish up the little bit that's left in a bunch of different jars in the fridge.

Black Forest Ice Cream Cake

You know the expression "Save the best for last"? Well, here's my interpretation.

One ½-gallon block chocolate ice cream

1 container (8 ounces) frozen whipped topping, thawed

1 container (21 ounces) cherry pie filling, drained

1 package (3 ounces) ladyfingers, each split in half

¼ cup miniature semisweet chocolate chips

Remove the block of ice cream from the package and place on a serving platter, then spread the whipped topping evenly over the sides. Spread the drained cherry pie filling over the top of the block, then stand the ladyfingers against the whipped topping, lining the outside of the ice cream block. Sprinkle the top with the chocolate chips and serve, or cover loosely and keep frozen until ready to serve.

HELPFUL HINT:
Draining the pie filling gives us the fruit with just a little of the gel so our dessert is extra fruity.

TO FANCY IT UP:
A tube of decorating gel will help turn this ice cream cake into a personalized birthday or anniversary cake.

DESSERT

152

Just-Your-Size Baked Alaska

1 package (6½ ounces) dessert shells
(6 shells)

1 pint strawberry ice cream

4 egg whites

½ cup sugar

Would you believe baked Alaska was actually invented by a scientist who was testing the effects of heating and cooling? Who knew a science experiment could taste so good . . . and be this easy, too!

Preheat the oven to 500°F. Place the dessert shells on a cookie sheet and scoop an equal amount of the ice cream into each one. Place in the freezer. In a medium bowl, beat the egg whites until foamy. Add the sugar and continue beating until stiff peaks form to make meringue. Remove the ice cream-filled dessert shells from the freezer and quickly spread the meringue over the ice cream and the sides of the dessert shells, coating completely. Bake for 2 to 4 minutes, or until the meringue is golden. Serve immediately.

> **HELPFUL HINT:**
> Watch these closely while baking—you want them to be nice and golden, but not burned. Oh—dessert shells can usually be found in the produce department of the supermarket, near the strawberries.

DESSERT

Banana Rockets

One of the easiest ways to get the kids to eat their fruits and veggies is to disguise them in foods they like—you know, like sprinkling veggies on top of pizza and covering them with cheese. How about this way—smothering bananas in chocolate and serving them frozen? What a sweet disguise.

3 bananas, peeled and cut crosswise in half

½ cup toasted coconut

1 cup (6 ounces) semisweet chocolate chips, melted

Line a baking sheet with waxed paper. Insert a wooden craft stick or skewer through the cut end of each banana half. Place the toasted coconut in a shallow dish. Spoon the melted chocolate over the bananas, covering them completely, then roll in the toasted coconut, coating completely. Place on the baking sheet and freeze for 10 minutes. Serve, or cover and keep frozen until ready to serve.

FOR A CHANGE OF PACE:
Use nuts, colored sprinkles, or miniature candies in place of the coconut to create your own special toppings.

HELPFUL HINT:
Toasting coconut is easy! Just spread it out on a rimmed baking sheet and toast in a 350°F. oven until golden . . . but be careful, because if you don't watch it, it will burn.

DESSERT

154

Brandied Peach Parfait

¼ cup (½ stick) butter
½ cup firmly packed light brown sugar
1 can (29 ounces) sliced peaches, drained
1 tablespoon brandy
1 quart vanilla ice cream

Fancy-up plain vanilla ice cream by adding brandied peaches and turning it into a good-to-the-last-spoonful parfait. It may not take long to make, but it sure is one dessert that'll get noticed.

Melt the butter in a large skillet over medium heat. Add the brown sugar and stir until thickened. Add the sliced peaches and stir to coat evenly. Remove from the heat and stir in the brandy. Place scoops of ice cream into bowls or parfait glasses and top with the brandied peach mixture. Serve immediately.

> **TO FANCY IT UP:**
> Make a brandied peach Melba that'll add even more color and flavor to your parfaits by mixing fresh raspberries in with the brandy at the last minute.

DESSERT

155

Instant Strawberry Sorbet

It's a steamy summer night and the gang is begging for an icy-cold dessert to beat the heat. Uh-oh, there's nothing in the freezer but a bag of frozen fruit. So, in less time than it would take to go to the store, we can whip up a creamy smooth sorbet that'll surely cool us off.

ABOUT 1 PINT

1 package (16 ounces) frozen strawberries

¾ cup light corn syrup

Combine the strawberries and corn syrup in a blender or food processor and blend until smooth. Serve immediately, or cover and freeze until ready to serve.

SO MANY OPTIONS!
Since variety is the spice of life, try this with different frozen fruits, from blueberries, raspberries, and blackberries to peaches.

Chilled Peaches 'n' Cream Soup

4 TO 6 SERVINGS

You might be thinking this recipe is in the wrong place, 'cause who ever heard of a dessert soup? Trust me, this creamy soup is the perfect light ending for a summer meal. One taste, and you'll be feeling really peachy.

2 cans (29 ounces each) sliced peaches in syrup, drained

1 cup milk

1 cup (½ pint) heavy cream

¼ cup sugar

1 teaspoon vanilla extract

In a blender or food processor, purée all the ingredients until smooth. Transfer to a large bowl; cover and freeze for 25 minutes. Serve, or refrigerate until ready to serve.

TO FANCY IT UP:
Garnish each serving with a dollop of lightly whipped cream and some thinly sliced peaches.

Fruit Stand Surprise

*There's nothing more refresh-
ing than a fresh fruit salad.
But let's face it; the same old
salad gets a little boring after
a while. That's why I came
up with this stuffed can-
taloupe. Not only is it easy to
make, it's easy on our eyes
and our taste buds, too.*

1 container (8 ounces)
vanilla yogurt

2 teaspoons light brown sugar

1 quart fresh strawberries, washed, hulled,
and sliced

2 bananas, peeled and sliced

2 kiwis, peeled and sliced

2 cantaloupes, quartered and seeded

2 tablespoons sliced almonds

In a large bowl, com-
bine the yogurt and
brown sugar; mix well.
Add the strawberries, bananas,
and kiwis; toss to mix well. Place
each cantaloupe quarter on a serving
plate. Spoon equal amounts of the fruit mixture over them and
top with the sliced almonds. Serve immediately.

DESSERT

FOR A CHANGE OF PACE:
Don't limit yourself to just vanilla yogurt. Try
cheesecake-flavored yogurt for a new fruit
salad taste.

Tortilla Crepes

4 SERVINGS

1 can (21 ounces) cherry pie filling, divided

Four 8-inch flour tortillas

1 tablespoon confectioners' sugar

½ cup frozen whipped topping, thawed

So we're in the mood for a little something sweet, like maybe a cherry pie. Well, in no time at all we can come up with something pretty darned close to that pie we're craving—and much easier to prepare.

Preheat the oven to 350°F. Reserve ¼ cup pie filling; spoon the remaining pie filling equally over the tortillas, forming a line across the center of each. Roll up and place seam side down on a baking sheet. Bake for 8 to 10 minutes, or until bubbly and heated through. Let cool for 5 minutes, then sprinkle with the confectioners' sugar. Top each with a dollop of both whipped topping and reserved pie filling. Serve warm.

FOR A CHANGE OF PACE:
Alternate between cherry, blueberry, apple, peach, and strawberry pie filling for a new flavor every time you make these.

DESSERT

159

Lightning-Quick Baklava

It takes hours to make traditional baklava, so when we don't have that much time, this shortcut version is ready quick as lightning. (And that's how fast it'll disappear from the table!)

25 SQUARES

1 sheet frozen puff pastry (from a 17¼-ounce package), thawed

1 cup chopped walnuts

¼ cup confectioners' sugar

¼ cup (½ stick) butter, melted

2 tablespoons light corn syrup

2 tablespoons honey

1 teaspoon fresh lemon juice

Preheat the oven to 400°F. On a lightly floured surface, roll out the puff pastry sheet to a 10-inch square, then cut into 2-inch squares; place on a baking sheet. In a small bowl, combine the walnuts, sugar, and butter; mix well. Spoon the mixture evenly into the centers of the squares. Bake for 12 to 14 minutes, or until the pastry is golden. In a small bowl, combine the corn syrup, honey, and lemon juice; mix well. Brush evenly over the tops of the hot pastry squares. Allow to cool on wire racks and serve, or store in a single layer in a large airtight container until ready to serve.

HELPFUL HINT:
If you're expecting a big crowd, you'd better bake a second batch with the second sheet of puff pastry. (Of course, double the other ingredients, too.)

Sweet Endings Pizza

12 TO 16 SLICES

You won't find this pizza on the menu at any pizzeria, but it's sure to become a regular on your table once your gang gets a taste!

1 package (18 ounces) refrigerated chocolate chip cookie dough
1 jar (7 ounces) marshmallow creme
½ cup M&M's
½ cup chopped peanuts

Preheat the oven to 350°F. Coat a 12-inch pizza pan with nonstick cooking spray. Cut the cookie dough into 24 slices and place on the pizza pan. With your fingers, press the dough together, forming one large cookie the size of the pan. Bake for 12 to 15 minutes, or until golden; allow to cool slightly. Spread the marshmallow creme over the cookie, leaving a ¼-inch border around the edge. Sprinkle with the candies and peanuts, then cut into wedges.

SO MANY OPTIONS!
As with any other pizza, feel free to add your favorite toppings. You can even spell out a birthday greeting or your favorite expression with the candies or a tube of decorating gel.

Orange Cocoa Sandies

Knock-knock. Who's there? Orange. Orange who? "Orange" ya glad these cookies are so simple to make and taste so yummy?

ABOUT 4 DOZEN COOKIES

1 cup (2 sticks) butter, softened

1¾ cups all-purpose flour

1¼ cups confectioners' sugar, divided

¼ cup unsweetened cocoa

1 cup finely chopped pecans

1 teaspoon orange extract

Preheat the oven to 400°F. In a large bowl, beat the butter, flour, 1 cup confectioners' sugar, the cocoa, pecans, and extract for 2 to 3 minutes, or until well blended. Drop by teaspoonfuls about 1 inch apart onto ungreased baking sheets. Bake for 8 to 10 minutes, or until set. Allow to cool slightly, then dust with the remaining ¼ cup confectioners' sugar. Serve, or store in an airtight container until ready to serve.

SO MANY OPTIONS!
For traditional pecan sandies, leave out the cocoa, change the orange extract to vanilla, and increase the flour to 2 cups.

Cocoa Peanut Drops

ABOUT 5 DOZEN CANDIES

When we're looking for a little something sweet to have with our after-dinner coffee, tea, or milk, these will do the trick. What a tasty treat!

2 cups sugar

½ cup unsweetened cocoa

½ cup half-and-half

5 tablespoons butter

1½ cups salted peanuts, coarsely chopped

1 cup old-fashioned or quick-cooking rolled oats

½ cup creamy peanut butter

1 teaspoon vanilla extract

Line a cookie sheet with waxed paper. In a medium saucepan, bring the sugar, cocoa, half-and-half, and butter to a boil over medium-high heat. Let boil for 2 minutes, stirring constantly. Remove from the heat and stir in the remaining ingredients; mix well. Drop by teaspoonfuls 1 inch apart onto the cookie sheet. Chill for 10 minutes, or until firm. Serve, or store in an airtight container until ready to serve.

FOR A CHANGE OF PACE:
Use cashews one time, macadamias another, or even roasted almonds or pecans in place of the peanuts.

DESSERT

163

Mocha Almond Truffles

After they taste these, everybody will think you spent a fortune at a fancy candy shop. Wait until they hear that you made 'em! Why, you'll be elected president of the local chocoholics' club.

2 tablespoons water

1 tablespoon instant coffee granules

¾ cup (4½ ounces) semisweet chocolate chips

¾ cup ground almonds

¾ cup confectioners' sugar, divided

In a medium saucepan, combine the water and coffee granules over medium heat, stirring until the coffee granules dissolve. Add the chocolate and stir until melted. Remove from the heat and stir in the almonds and ½ cup confectioners' sugar until firm. Shape into 2 dozen 1-inch balls, then roll in the remaining ¼ cup confectioners' sugar. Place on a baking sheet and chill for 10 minutes, or until firm. Serve, or store in an airtight container until ready to serve.

TO FANCY IT UP:
Coat some of the truffles with cocoa and others with sprinkles or colored sugar. That adds a variety of color and flavor to them.

Rocky Road Popcorn Balls

2 DOZEN POPCORN BALLS

Kids aren't the only ones who deserve a sweet treat inside their lunch boxes. Why not secretly mix up a batch of these popcorn balls, then surprise the family by sneaking one into everybody's lunch bags?

3 tablespoons butter

1 package (10 ounces) marshmallows

14 cups popped popcorn

1 cup salted peanuts

1 package (7 ounces) chocolate-covered raisins

Melt the butter in a soup pot over low heat. Add the marshmallows and stir until melted. Remove from the heat and add the popcorn and peanuts; stir until completely coated. Add the chocolate-covered raisins; mix well. Form into 2 dozen balls and serve, or store in an airtight container until ready to serve.

HELPFUL HINTS:
Coat your hands with nonstick cooking spray to keep the marshmallow mixture from sticking to them when forming the balls. Two packages of microwave popcorn should yield about 14 cups of popcorn.

almond:
   mocha truffles, 164
   -raspberry-mocha torte, 151
almost lobster tail, 133
angel food cake, tropical, 149
antipasto, big bowl, 47
apple cider fondue, cheesy, 68
apple pie toast, 7
arepas, easy, 64
artichoke-crab pizza wedges,
   84
awesome freezer s'mores, 75

bacon 'n' cheese bites, 79
baked Alaska, just-your-size, 153
baked chocolate chip pancakes,
   29
baklava, lightning-quick, 160
banana(s):
   -chocolate baked French toast,
   28
   grilled PBM&Bs, 60
   rockets, 154
bandito burrito bake, 26
barbecue:
   blue chips, 81
   chicken sandwiches, 54
   country ribs, 104
beans:
   'n' franks soup, 37

twenty-minute Italian chili,
   102
beef:
   beat-the-clock goulash, 99
   chipped, creamed, 24
   ground, see ground meats
   lower-fat preparation of,
   xv–xvi
   mustard steak salad, 124
   orange teriyaki, 96
   porterhouse for two, 123
   quick-as-a-wink stew, 95
   roast, "crepes," 94
   steak 'n' potato soup, 36
beer dip, cheesy, 77
beverages:
   mocha icee, 13
   shortcut fresh OJ, 31
   super-smooth smoothie, 71
big bowl antipasto, 47
biscuits with sausage gravy, 25
bites, bacon 'n' cheese, 79
bite-sized Mexican pizzas, 80
Black Forest ice cream cake, 152
blue chips, barbecue, 81
brandied peach parfait, 155
breads:
   apple pie toast, 7
   baked chocolate chip
      pancakes, 29
   biscuits with sausage gravy, 25

breads (*continued*)
   chocolate-banana baked
      French toast, 28
   cinnamon pecan muffins, 12
   French toast sticks, 5
   morning pizza, 6
   open-faced strawberry cheese
      Danish, 30
   pecan sticky buns, 27
   pesto chicken bruschetta, 85
   pizza crisps, 76
   raspberry toaster cakes, 10
   sausage pancake muffins, 11
   white pita pizza, 86
breakfast, 3–13
   apple pie toast, 7
   cinnamon pecan muffins, 12
   cookies, 9
   French toast sticks, 5
   mocha icee, 13
   morning pizza, 6
   raspberry toaster cakes, 10
   sausage pancake muffins, 11
   3-2-1 power bars, 8
brunch, 15–31
   baked chocolate chip
      pancakes, 29
   bandito burrito bake, 26
   biscuits with sausage gravy,
      25
   bull's-eye eggs, 23
   chocolate-banana baked
      French toast, 28
   crab puffs, 19
   creamed chipped beef, 24
   mini ham and cheese quiches,
      18

   open-faced strawberry cheese
      Danish, 30
   pecan sticky buns, 27
   shortcut fresh OJ, 31
   shortcut omelets, 22
   skillet home fries and eggs,
      21
   vegetable frittata, 20
bruschetta, pesto chicken, 85
Buffalo chicken tenders, 82
bull's-eye eggs, 23
buns, sticky, pecan, 27
burrito:
   bandito bake, 26
   chicken soup, 38

Caesar salad, chicken, 129
cakes:
   Black Forest ice cream, 152
   raspberry toaster, 10
   strawberry patch shortcake,
      143
   tropical angel food, 149
   upside-down strawberry
      cheesecake, 147
calzones, curried chicken, 57
candy:
   cocoa peanut drops, 163
   mocha almond truffles, 164
   peanut butter–chocolate, 72
   rocky road popcorn balls, 165
caramel swirl chocolate pie, 145
carrot cake cookies, 67
cheese(y):
   apple cider fondue, 68
   beer dip, 77

chicken cordon bleu
        sandwiches, 55
chicken quesadillas, 56
easy arepas, 64
fish parmigiana, 113
and ham quiches, mini, 18
lower-fat, xiii–xiv
'n' bacon bites, 79
one-pot macaroni and, 118
open-faced strawberry Danish,
        30
pesto chicken bruschetta, 85
potato soup, 40
skillet chicken noodle
        parmigiana, 111
tuna melt soup, 39
cheeseburger bake, 98
cheesecake, upside-down
        strawberry, 147
chicken:
    barbecue sandwiches, 54
    Buffalo tenders, 82
    burrito soup, 38
    Caesar salad, 129
    cordon bleu sandwiches, 55
    curried calzones, 57
    fancy fast Greek, 105
    francaise, quick, 128
    lower-fat preparation of, xiii
    noodle parmigiana, skillet, 111
    off-the-skewer kebabs, 135
    pesto bruschetta, 85
    pesto salad, grilled, 42
    Polynesian, 106
    and potato salad, 44
    quesadillas, 56
    vegetable penne, 107

chili, twenty-minute Italian,
        102
chilled soups:
    peaches 'n' cream, 157
    shrimp cocktail, 41
chipped beef, creamed, 24
chips:
    barbecue blue, 81
    crispy fish 'n', 108
    piled-high nachos, 83
chocolate:
    -banana baked French toast,
        28
    caramel swirl pie, 145
    -peanut butter candy, 72
    peanut butter pretzels, 73
    raspberry soufflé, 146
    white, macadamia mousse,
        150
chocolate chip(s):
    baked pancakes, 29
    banana rockets, 154
    ice cream sandwiches, 74
    mocha almond truffles, 164
    peanut butter cup roll-ups, 65
cider, apple, cheesy fondue, 68
cinnamon:
    pecan muffins, 12
    -sugar pretzels, 69
    -toast popcorn, 87
clambake, skillet, 131
clams scampi, 116
Cobb salad, 46
cocoa:
    orange sandies, 162
    peanut drops, 163
coffee makers, cleaning of, 26

cookies:
  breakfast, 9
  carrot cake, 67
  orange cocoa sandies, 162
  sweet-and-salty, 66
cordon bleu chicken
      sandwiches, 55
Cornish hens, fruity, 130
country barbecue ribs, 104
country-French patties, 97
couscous, vegetable, 119
crab:
  -artichoke pizza wedges, 84
  creamy casserole, 112
  puffs, 19
cream:
  lemon tarts, 148
  peaches 'n', chilled soup, 157
  sour, low-fat, xiv
  whipped, low-fat, xiv
cream cheese, low-fat, xiii
creamed chipped beef, 24
creamy crab casserole, 112
"crepes," roast beef, 94
crepes, tortilla, 159
crisps, pizza, 76
crispy fish 'n' chips, 108
croissants, shrimp salad, 58
curried chicken calzones, 57

dairy products, lower-fat
      preparation of, xiii–xiv
Danish, open-faced strawberry
      cheese, 30
dessert, 139–165
  banana rockets, 154

Black Forest ice cream cake,
  152
brandied peach parfait, 155
chilled peaches 'n' cream
  soup, 157
chocolate caramel swirl pie,
  145
chocolate raspberry soufflé,
  146
cocoa peanut drops, 163
fruit stand surprise, 158
instant strawberry sorbet, 156
just-your-size baked Alaska,
  153
lemon cream tarts, 148
lightning-quick baklava, 160
mocha almond truffles, 164
orange cocoa sandies, 162
pink lemonade pie, 144
raspberry-almond-mocha
  torte, 151
rocky road popcorn balls, 165
strawberry patch shortcake,
  143
sweet endings pizza, 161
tortilla crepes, 159
tropical angel food cake, 149
upside-down strawberry
  cheesecake, 147
white chocolate macadamia
  mousse, 150
Dijon marmalade pork chops,
  103
dinner, family, *see* family dinner
dinner for two, 121–137
  almost lobster tail, 133
  chicken Caesar salad, 129

fruity Cornish hens, 130
herb-crusted rack of lamb, 126
mustard steak salad, 124
off-the-skewer chicken
    kebabs, 135
pork tenderloin marsala, 127
porterhouse, 123
potato-crusted salmon, 132
quick chicken francaise, 128
sizzlin' shrimp stir-fry, 134
skillet clambake, 131
spinach fettuccine primavera,
    136
tortellini with portobello
    mushrooms, 137
veal alla Patty, 125
dip, cheesy beer, 77
dressings, low-fat, xiv
drinks, *see* beverages
drops, cocoa peanut, 163

easy arepas, 64
egg rolls, Oriental salad, 59
eggs:
    bull's-eye, 23
    shortcut omelets, 22
    skillet home fries and, 21
    substitutions for, xiv
    vegetable frittata, 20

family dinner, 89–119
    beat-the-clock goulash, 99
    cheeseburger bake, 98
    chicken vegetable penne,
        107

clams scampi, 116
country barbecue ribs, 104
country-French patties, 97
creamy crab casserole, 112
crispy fish 'n' chips, 108
fancy fast Greek chicken, 105
fish parmigiana, 113
gobble-it-up spaghetti, 109
marmalade Dijon pork chops,
    103
one-pot macaroni and cheese,
    118
orange beef teriyaki, 96
Parmesan turkey meat loaves,
    110
Polynesian chicken, 106
quick-as-a-wink beef stew, 95
ravioli cacciatore, 100
roast beef "crepes," 94
shrimp "fried" rice, 114
skillet chicken noodle
    parmigiana, 111
smothered pork chops, 101
spinach pasta soufflé, 117
stovetop meat loaves, 93
stovetop tuna casserole, 115
twenty-minute Italian chili,
    102
vegetable couscous, 119
fancy fast Greek chicken, 105
fettuccine, spinach, primavera,
    136
fish:
    almost lobster tail, 133
    'n' chips, crispy, 108
    parmigiana, 113
    potato-crusted salmon, 132

fish (*continued*)
  stovetop tuna casserole, 115
  tuna melt soup, 39
fondue, cheesy apple cider, 68
franks, *see* hot dog(s)
freezer s'mores, awesome, 75
French country patties, 97
French toast:
  chocolate-banana baked, 28
  sticks, 5
"fried" rice, shrimp, 114
frittata, vegetable, 20
frozen sweets:
  awesome freezer s'mores, 75
  banana rockets, 154
  Black Forest ice cream cake, 152
  brandied peach parfait, 155
  chilled peaches 'n' cream
    soup, 157
  chocolate chip ice cream
    sandwiches, 74
  instant strawberry sorbet, 156
  just-your-size baked Alaska,
    153
  pink lemonade pie, 144
fruit roll sushi, 70
fruit stand surprise, 158
fruity Cornish hens, 130

gobble-it-up spaghetti, 109
goulash, beat-the-clock, 99
gravy, sausage, biscuits with, 25
Greek chicken, fancy fast, 105
grilled foods:
  PBM&Bs, 60
  pesto chicken salad, 42

ground meats:
  beat-the-clock goulash, 99
  biscuits with sausage gravy,
    25
  cheeseburger bake, 98
  country-French patties, 97
  gobble-it-up turkey spaghetti,
    109
  lower-fat preparation of,
    xv–xvi
  Parmesan turkey meat loaves,
    110
  sausage pancake muffins, 11
  stovetop meat loaves, 93
  twenty-minute Italian chili,
    102

ham:
  and cheese quiches, mini, 18
  chicken cordon bleu
    sandwiches, 55
  join-the-club tortilla, 52
hamburgers, *see* ground meats
Hawaiian stuffed pizza, 51
herb-crusted rack of lamb, 126
home fries and eggs, skillet, 21
hot dog(s):
  franks 'n' beans soup, 37
  puffs, 78
  Reubens, 50

ice cream:
  awesome freezer s'mores, 75
  Black Forest cake, 152
  brandied peach parfait, 155

chocolate chip sandwiches, 74
just-your-size baked Alaska,
    153
icee, mocha, 13
instant strawberry sorbet, 156

join-the-club tortilla, 52
just-your-size baked Alaska, 153

kebabs, off-the-skewer chicken,
    135

lamb, herb-crusted rack of, 126
lemonade, pink, pie, 144
lemon cream tarts, 148
lightning-quick baklava, 160
lobster tail, almost, 133
lower-fat cooking, xiii–xvii
lunch, 33–60
    barbecue chicken sandwiches,
        54
    big bowl antipasto, 47
    cheese potato soup, 40
    chicken and potato salad, 44
    chicken burrito soup, 38
    chicken cordon bleu
        sandwiches, 55
    chicken quesadillas, 56
    chilled shrimp cocktail soup,
        41
    Cobb salad, 46
    curried chicken calzones, 57
    franks 'n' beans soup, 37
    grilled PBM&Bs, 60

    grilled pesto chicken salad,
        42
    Hawaiian stuffed pizza, 51
    hot dog Reubens, 50
    join-the-club tortilla, 52
    Oriental salad egg rolls, 59
    Philly pita, lunch box, 49
    quiche Lorraine salad, 45
    shrimp salad croissants, 58
    smoked turkey sandwiches,
        53
    stacked tomato, 48
    steak 'n' potato soup, 36
    taco salad pie, 43
    tuna melt soup, 3

macadamia white chocolate
    mousse, 150
macaroni and cheese, one-pot,
    118
marmalade Dijon pork chops,
    103
marsala, pork tenderloin, 127
mayonnaise, light, xv
meat loaves:
    Parmesan turkey, 110
    stovetop, 93
mini ham and cheese quiches,
    18
mocha:
    almond truffles, 164
    icee, 13
    -raspberry-almond torte, 151
monkfish, almost lobster tail,
    133
morning pizza, 6

mousse, white chocolate
    macadamia, 150
mozzarella cheese, low-fat, xiii
muffins:
    cinnamon pecan, 12
    sausage pancake, 11
munchies, *see* snacks
mushrooms, portobello,
    tortellini with, 137
mustard steak salad, 124

nachos, piled-high, 83
noodle parmigiana, skillet
    chicken, 111
nuts:
    cutting down amounts of, xvi
    see also specific nuts

off-the-skewer chicken kebabs,
    135
oils, lower-fat, xvi
OJ, shortcut fresh, 31
omelets, shortcut, 22
one-pot macaroni and cheese,
    118
open-faced strawberry cheese
    Danish, 30
orange beef teriyaki, 96
orange cocoa sandies, 162
orange juice, shortcut fresh, 31
Oriental salad egg rolls, 59

packaged foods, xvii
pancake muffins, sausage, 11

pancakes, baked chocolate chip,
    29
parfait, brandied peach, 155
Parmesan cheese:
    low-fat, xiii
    turkey meat loaves, 110
pasta:
    chicken vegetable penne,
        107
    clams scampi, 116
    gobble-it-up spaghetti, 109
    one-pot macaroni and cheese,
        118
    ravioli cacciatore, 100
    skillet chicken noodle
        parmigiana, 111
    spinach fettuccine primavera,
        136
    spinach soufflé, 117
    stovetop tuna casserole, 115
    tortellini with portobello
        mushrooms, 137
patties, country-French, 97
Patty, veal alla, 125
PBM&Bs, grilled, 60
peach(es):
    brandied parfait, 155
    'n' cream soup, chilled, 157
peanut butter:
    –chocolate candy, 72
    chocolate pretzels, 73
    cocoa drops, 163
    cup roll-ups, 65
    grilled PBM&Bs, 60
pecan:
    cinnamon muffins, 12
    sticky buns, 27

penne, chicken vegetable, 107
pesto:
  chicken bruschetta, 85
  chicken salad, grilled, 42
Philly pita, lunch box, 49
pies:
  apple toast, 7
  chocolate caramel swirl, 145
  pink lemonade, 144
  taco salad, 43
piled-high nachos, 83
pink lemonade pie, 144
pita:
  lunch box Philly, 49
  white pizza, 86
pizza(s):
  artichoke-crab wedges, 84
  bite-sized Mexican, 80
  crisps, 76
  Hawaiian stuffed, 51
  morning, 6
  sweet endings, 161
  white pita, 86
Polynesian chicken, 106
popcorn, cinnamon-toast, 87
popcorn balls, rocky road, 165
pork:
  country barbecue ribs, 104
  lower-fat preparation of,
    xv–xvi
  tenderloin marsala, 127
pork chops:
  marmalade Dijon, 103
  smothered, 101
porterhouse for two, 123
portobello mushrooms,
    tortellini with, 137

potato(es):
  cheese soup, 40
  and chicken salad, 44
  -crusted salmon, 132
  skillet home fries and eggs,
    21
  'n' steak soup, 36
potato chips:
  barbecue blue, 81
  crispy fish 'n', 108
power bars, 3–2–1, 8
pretzels:
  chocolate peanut butter, 73
  cinnamon-sugar, 69
  sweet-and-salty cookies, 66
primavera, spinach fettuccine,
    136
puffs:
  bacon 'n' cheese bites, 79
  crab, 19
  hot dog, 78

quesadillas, chicken, 56
quiches:
  Lorraine, salad, 45
  mini ham and cheese, 18
quick-as-a-wink beef stew, 95
quick chicken francaise, 128

rack of lamb, herb-crusted, 126
raspberry:
  -almond-mocha torte, 151
  chocolate soufflé, 146
  toaster cakes, 10
ravioli cacciatore, 100

Reubens, hot dog, 50
ribs, country barbecue, 104
rice, shrimp "fried," 114
ricotta cheese, low-fat, xiv
roast beef "crepes," 94
rockets, banana, 154
rocky road popcorn balls, 165

salads, 42–48
    big bowl antipasto, 47
    chicken and potato, 44
    chicken Caesar, 129
    Cobb, 46
    grilled pesto chicken, 42
    low-fat dressings for, xiv
    mustard steak, 124
    Oriental, egg rolls, 59
    quiche Lorraine, 45
    shrimp, croissants, 58
    stacked tomato, 48
    taco pie, 43
salmon, potato-crusted, 132
sandies, orange cocoa, 162
sandwiches, 49–60
    awesome freezer s'mores,
        75
    barbecue chicken, 54
    chicken cordon bleu, 55
    chicken quesadillas, 56
    chocolate chip ice cream, 74
    curried chicken calzones, 57
    grilled PBM&Bs, 60
    Hawaiian stuffed pizza, 51
    hot dog Reubens, 50
    join-the-club tortilla, 52
    lunch box Philly pita, 49

Oriental salad egg rolls, 59
    shrimp salad croissants, 58
    smoked turkey, 53
sauces, healthier preparation of,
    xvi
sausage(s):
    franks 'n' beans soup, 37
    gravy, biscuits with, 25
    hot dog puffs, 78
    hot dog Reubens, 50
    lower-fat, xvi
    pancake muffins, 11
    turkey, gobble-it-up spaghetti,
        109
    twenty-minute Italian chili,
        102
scampi, clams, 116
shellfish:
    artichoke-crab pizza wedges,
        84
    chilled shrimp cocktail soup,
        41
    clams scampi, 116
    crab puffs, 19
    creamy crab casserole, 112
    shrimp "fried" rice, 114
    shrimp salad croissants, 58
    sizzlin' shrimp stir-fry, 134
    skillet clambake, 131
shortcake, strawberry patch, 143
shortcut fresh OJ, 31
shortcut omelets, 22
shrimp:
    cocktail, chilled soup, 41
    "fried" rice, 114
    salad croissants, 58
    sizzlin' stir-fry, 134

skillet dishes:
  chicken noodle parmigiana,
    111
  clambake, 131
  home fries and eggs, 21
smoked turkey sandwiches, 53
smoothies:
  mocha icee, 13
  super-smooth, 71
s'mores, awesome freezer, 75
smothered pork chops, 101
snacks, 61–87
  artichoke-crab pizza wedges,
    84
  awesome freezer s'mores, 75
  bacon 'n' cheese bites, 79
  barbecue blue chips, 81
  bite-sized Mexican pizzas, 80
  Buffalo chicken tenders, 82
  carrot cake cookies, 67
  cheesy apple cider fondue,
    68
  cheesy beer dip, 77
  chocolate chip ice cream
    sandwiches, 74
  chocolate peanut butter
    pretzels, 73
  cinnamon-sugar pretzels, 69
  cinnamon-toast popcorn, 87
  easy arepas, 64
  fruit roll sushi, 70
  hot dog puffs, 78
  peanut butter–chocolate
    candy, 72
  peanut butter cup roll-ups,
    65
  pesto chicken bruschetta, 85

  piled-high nachos, 83
  pizza crisps, 76
  super-smooth smoothie, 71
  sweet-and-salty cookies, 66
  white pita pizza, 86
  see also lunch
sorbet, instant strawberry, 156
soufflés:
  chocolate raspberry, 146
  spinach pasta, 117
soups, 36–41
  cheese potato, 40
  chicken burrito, 38
  chilled, see chilled soups
  franks 'n' beans, 37
  healthier preparation of, xv,
    xvii
  steak 'n' potato, 36
  tuna melt, 39
sour cream, low-fat, xiv
spaghetti, gobble-it-up, 109
spinach fettuccine primavera,
    136
spinach pasta soufflé, 117
stacked tomato salad, 48
steak:
  mustard salad, 124
  porterhouse for two, 123
  'n' potato soup, 36
stews:
  beat-the-clock goulash, 99
  quick-as-a-wink beef, 95
sticks, French toast, 5
sticky buns, pecan, 27
stir-fry, sizzlin' shrimp, 134
stovetop meat loaves, 93
stovetop tuna casserole, 115

strawberry:
    cheese Danish, open-faced, 30
    instant sorbet, 156
    upside-down cheesecake, 147
strawberry patch shortcake, 143
sugar-cinnamon pretzels, 69
super-smooth smoothie, 71
surprise, fruit stand, 158
sushi, fruit roll, 70
sweet-and-salty cookies, 66
sweet endings pizza, 161

taco salad pie, 43
tarts, lemon cream, 148
tenders, Buffalo chicken, 82
teriyaki, orange beef, 96
3-2-1 power bars, 8
toast:
    apple pie, 7
    French, chocolate-banana
        baked, 28
    French, sticks, 5
toaster cakes, raspberry, 10
tomato salad, stacked, 48
torte, raspberry-almond-mocha,
    151
tortellini with portobello
    mushrooms, 137
tortilla:
    crepes, 159
    join-the-club, 52
tropical angel food cake, 149
truffles, mocha almond, 164

tuna:
    casserole, stovetop, 115
    melt soup, 39
turkey:
    ground, xvi
    join-the-club tortilla, 52
    Parmesan meat loaves, 110
    sausage, gobble-it-up
        spaghetti, 109
    smoked, sandwiches, 53
twenty-minute Italian chili, 102

upside-down strawberry
    cheesecake, 147

veal alla Patty, 125
vegetable(s):
    chicken penne, 107
    couscous, 119
    frittata, 20
    spinach fettuccine primavera,
        136

whipped cream, low-fat, xiv
white chocolate macadamia
    mousse, 150
white pita pizza, 86

yogurt:
    fruit stand surprise, 158
    and mayonnaise, xv
    super-smooth smoothie, 71

A

B

C

D

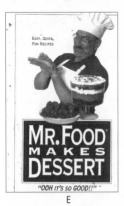

E

F

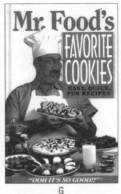

G

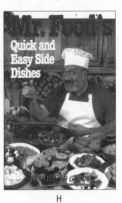

H

I

J

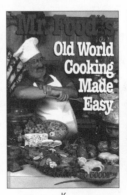

K

L

M

N

O

P

Mr. Food®'s Library Gives You More Ways to Say . . . "OOH IT'S SO GOOD!!®"

WILLIAM MORROW

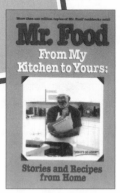

Q

R

S

T

U

V

W

X

Y

Mr. Food ® CAN HELP YOU BE A KITCHEN HERO!

Let **Mr. Food** ® make your life easier with Quick, No-Fuss Recipes and Helpful Kitchen Tips for

Family Dinners • Soups and Salads • Potluck Dishes • Barbecues • Special Brunches • Unbelievable Desserts

. . . and that's just the beginning!

Complete your **Mr. Food** ® cookbook library today. It's so simple to share in all the **"OOH IT'S SO GOOD!!®"**

✂- -

TITLE	PRICE	QUANTITY	
A. **Mr. Food** ® Cooks Like Mama	@ $14.95 each	x _____	= $_____
B. The **Mr. Food** ® Cookbook, *OOH IT'S SO GOOD!!* ®	@ $14.95 each	x _____	= $_____
C. **Mr. Food** ® Cooks Chicken	@ $11.95 each	x _____	= $_____
D. **Mr. Food** ® Cooks Pasta	@ $11.95 each	x _____	= $_____
E. **Mr. Food** ® Makes Dessert	@ $11.95 each	x _____	= $_____
F. **Mr. Food** ® Cooks Real American	@ $14.95 each	x _____	= $_____
G. **Mr. Food** ®'s Favorite Cookies	@ $11.95 each	x _____	= $_____
H. **Mr. Food** ®'s Quick and Easy Side Dishes	@ $11.95 each	x _____	= $_____
I. **Mr. Food** ® Grills It All in a Snap	@ $11.95 each	x _____	= $_____
J. **Mr. Food** ®'s Fun Kitchen Tips and Shortcuts (and Recipes, Too!)	@ $14.95 each	x _____	= $_____
K. **Mr. Food** ®'s Old World Cooking Made Easy	@ $14.95 each	x _____	= $_____
L. "Help, **Mr. Food** ®! Company's Coming!"	@ $14.95 each	x _____	= $_____
M. **Mr. Food** ® Pizza 1-2-3	@ $12.00 each	x _____	= $_____
N. **Mr. Food** ® Meat Around the Table	@ $12.00 each	x _____	= $_____
O. **Mr. Food** ® Simply Chocolate	@ $12.00 each	x _____	= $_____
P. **Mr. Food** ® A Little Lighter	@ $14.95 each	x _____	= $_____
Q. **Mr. Food** ® From My Kitchen to Yours: Stories and Recipes from Home	@ $14.95 each	x _____	= $_____
R. **Mr. Food** ® Easy Tex-Mex	@ $11.95 each	x _____	= $_____
S. **Mr. Food** ® One Pot, One Meal	@ $11.95 each	x _____	= $_____
T. **Mr. Food** ® Cool Cravings: Easy Chilled and Frozen Desserts	@ $11.95 each	x _____	= $_____
U. **Mr. Food** ®'s Italian Kitchen	@ $14.95 each	x _____	= $_____
V. **Mr. Food** ®'s Simple Southern Favorites	@ $14.95 each	x _____	= $_____
W. A **Mr. Food** ® Christmas: Homemade and Hassle-Free	@ $19.95 each	x _____	= $_____
X. **Mr. Food** ® Cooking by the Calendar	@ $14.95 each	x _____	= $_____
Y. **Mr. Food** ®'s Meals in Minutes	@ $14.95 each	x _____	= $_____
Z. **Mr. Food** ®'s Good Times, Good Food Cookbook	@ $14.95 each	x _____	= $_____
A A. **Mr. Food** ®'s Restaurant Favorites	@ $14.95 each	x _____	= $_____

Send payment to:
Mr. Food ®
P.O. Box 9227
Coral Springs, FL 33075-9227

Book Total $_____

+ Postage & Handling for *First Copy* $ **4.00**

+ $1 Postage & Handling for Ea. Add'l. Copy
(Canadian Orders Add Add'l. $2.00 *Per Copy*) $_____

Name _____

Street _____ Apt._____   **Subtotal** $_____

City _____ State_____ Zip_____
BKY

Add 6% Sales Tax
(FL Residents Only) $_____

Method of Payment Enclosed ☐ Check or ☐ Money Order

Please allow up to 6 weeks for delivery.   **Total in U.S. Funds** $_____

Like My Cookbooks?
Then You'll Love My Magazine!

Hot Off the Press...
Mr. Food's
EasyCooking
magazine

Soon you'll
be saying,
"OOH IT'S SO GOOD!!®"

**Look for it at your
local supermarket
or newsstand**

**Also available for $4
postpaid from
Hearst Single Copies,
P.O. Box 10577,
Des Moines, IA 50340
Or call: 1-800-925-0485
For subscriptions, call: 1-800-444-8783**